Sweardagod

by

Ben Sherman

FOR MY FRIENDS
BILL & JANET
WITH LOVE

Ben Sherman

Sweardagod

FIRST EDITION
FIRST PRINTING

Printed in the United States of America
Cielo Press, Washington

ISBN # 0-9644164-2-5

Cover Art: FootSteps Design
Cover Photo: Nick Vedros

Autobiographical Nonfiction
Some names of people and places have been changed.

Other books by Ben Sherman

Medic! The Story of a Conscientious Objector in the Vietnam War, Presidio Press, Random House, 2004.

Restore Breathing, Sherman Training, 1997

Table of Contents

Preface

My wife started reading to our children the day her first pregnancy test came back positive. Before our daughter arrived, she read constantly, every night, always aloud. Once she had a real live baby, she bought beautifully illustrated fairy tales and nursery rhymes. When our second daughter arrived, we celebrated by buying more picture books. As they advanced to children's stories and eventually chapter books, snug in their beds every night, their mom read to them without fail. They learned early that good books go together with warmth, safety, and love.

They heard stories from me too, but not the written kind. My daughters and I were together a lot since I worked out of our home and served as primary care-giver before and after school. Our family observed a weeknight ban on television, so the girls often had daddy for their entertainment.

"Tell us about being Goofy at Disneyland."

"I want to hear about the cows in the snow."

"Goofy at Disneyland!"

"Cows in the snow!"

"If you set the table for dinner, I'll tell you a quick story. Your mom will be home soon.

Raising kids requires bartering.

"GOOFY!!"

"COWS!!"

"Here's one you haven't heard."

"Is it a *true* story, Daddy?"

"Of course. Always."

In *Ethics,* Aristotle asks, "How should a human being lead his life?"

A good story answers his question. Whether as a play, movie or book, a well-crafted tale informs us how to live.

Following are stories I told my daughters.

For Star and Jen

Buddies

Right before my third birthday, we moved next door to a family who had been there only a few months. They had a son just a year older than I and, before our parents put in lawns and shrubbery, the two of us enjoyed small-boy heaven in the endless dirt around our houses. Much of my early story weaves through his.

As his uncompromising measure of truth, David demanded, "You sweardagod?" If I fibbed while invoking this solemn vow, I'd be doomed to an eternity standing on my head in a cesspool of snot and dog poop. In all our years growing up together, I never once invoked "sweardagod" in response to anything he told me. It always worked the other way. After all, he was three hundred and fifty-seven days older.

Dave Anderson was born to be an engineer. He included me in his experiments and construction projects, starting with roads and bridges for our trucks. We moved on to complicated electric train panoramas and several classic soapbox cars, a tandem bike, a river raft, a four-foot deep mud pit, a two-story fort, the neighborhood's first sitting lawnmower, and a sailboat built from a kit in Dave's garage.

I was inquisitive and much more of a dreamer than Dave. I followed my heart and intuition. He followed the directions.

Our parents wondered who offered the worst or best influence on the other. I would have to confess that, most of the time, I got us in trouble and David got us out.

The following are short stories about our early days as two energetic boys growing up together in a place where all the parents watched everybody else's kids, but none of them had any idea what we were really doing.

Busted

Our dads wouldn't allow us to have BB guns. It seemed like everybody else our age had one, but past transgressions had made our fathers wary. Beg as we might, the argument finally ended with threats that if we brought up the subject again we'd be chopping wood until college.

Boys need to shoot stuff. No one knows why. Dave and I launched marbles with slingshots and flung apples or lemons with a sling like the one David used to smack Goliath, but nothing matched an actual Red Rider BB Gun. Having lost the battle to get our own, we borrowed two guns from my friend Terry and headed out on a bike safari to get as far away from home as we could. Thus began our great hunt for animals small enough to be felled by a single BB. None presented themselves. The hand-pump rifles were so weak that you could see the copper shot leaving the end of the barrel. We cocked the guns fifteen times to try to get some velocity, but our first and last experience with weapons dissolved into aiming at empty cans propped up on a log.

"They keep falling short," I complained.

"Aim high. Give it an arc," David suggested.

We didn't know that kids played in a field right below our firing range. One of the BBs struck something near them, they scrambled home, and a mom called the police. After we'd been hitting nothing for about twenty minutes, two uniformed policemen appeared out of nowhere.

"What are your names, boys?"

11

"Benny."

"David John Anderson, sir."

"Where do you live?"

"Twenty one oh eight, Murieta Way, sir."

"Twenty one oh four."

"You live next door?"

"Yes, sir."

"You shootin' at kids?"

"No, sir."

"These your guns?"

"No, sir."

"Whose guns are they?"

"My friend Terry's."

"What you shooting at?"

"Those cans right over there."

He and his partner walked to where the cans were still sitting on the log. We hadn't hit any. They looked over the bluff to the gully below, back at us, then over the side again.

"Uh huh. I see."

"Yep."

"OK, then ..."

They locked us in the back seat of their patrol car as they continued to inspect the landscape. They probably understood what happened, but they couldn't have kids shooting guns into the general population no matter how far from houses we were. So Terry's guns and our two bikes went into the trunk, and we suffered a long ride home.

I whispered to Dave that I was scared. He put his finger to his lips.

"My dad will kill me," I murmured.

Dave again indicated for me to shut up. He looked more serious than I had ever seen him. I waited as long as I could.

"What will I tell Terry about his guns?"

"Shhh."

"Come on. What're we gonna do?"

"I'm thinking. Shut up."

I couldn't stay still. Just as I began to speak again, Dave looked at me in a very earnest way and said, "When we get home, just follow what I do. Don't say nuthin'."

The patrol car pulled up in front of our houses. The two policemen got out and opened our doors. David walked with his head down, directly toward *my* house! I stood and watched for a moment as the driver followed him. His partner took my elbow and headed me toward Dave's house. I obediently followed, saying nothing.

Mrs. Anderson answered the door and asked the officer to come in.

"Hello, Ben." Mrs. Anderson said to me with a questioning look.

"I'm Officer Thompson, ma'am."

"Ruth Anderson," she politely responded.

"We are here because your son and the neighbor boy have been shooting BB guns, and we received a complaint."

"Were you shooting at people?" Mrs. Anderson asked me.

I shook my head back and forth not daring to utter a sound.

"Where were they?" she asked the officer.

"Down by the river," he answered.

"Away from the houses?" she asked.

"Yes ma'am. They might not have seen the boys. But these BBs can go every which way. They need to be more careful."

"Thank you, officer. I will be sure to tell my son."

"Now would be a good time for that," the officer said. "I would like to hear your conversation with him. Then I'll be on my way."

"Right now?" she asked.

"Yes, ma'am. It would wrap this up for me."

"I'm sorry, Officer Thompson, that would be impossible at the moment."

Ruth began smiling in spite of her attempts not to.

"It would?"

Taken aback, he looked at her more closely. She smiled sweetly, almost laughing. He saw her expression and must have mistaken her response.

"And *why,* may I ask ma'am, would that be impossible? I'm sure you will agree that it is very important for parents to take responsibility for their children's behavior."

"Sir, I cannot tell my son …"

"Mrs. Anderson, you don't seem to understand. This is a serious thing."

"Mr. Thompson, *you* don't understand. This is not my son."

By now I had a smile that would not go away for days.

Dave and the other officer crossed our paths as Thompson and I walked to my house. Neither officer spoke to each other. We met my mom at the door.

"Mrs. Sherman?" he asked.

"Yes?"

"Is this your son?"

"Yes."

My mother held back her laughter as long as she could. When the officer finally broke into a big grin, she giggled out loud. That set him off too.

Sweardagod.

"Go to your room," my mom said through her giggles.

"Son," the officer asked, "Tell me again who owns those guns."

"Terry" I said.

I heard my mom give Terry's last name and address to the officer as I walked down the hall to my room. Nothing came of it. Terry got his guns back and, as far as Dave and I knew, our dads never found out. If they did, we couldn't hear them laughing.

Oscar

One set of parents wouldn't suffice on Murieta Way. I had three. Across the street, Lil Weinberg kept a steady eye on the doings of her son Steven. That meant she watched David and me as well. Ruth Anderson had been in cahoots with my mom since the day after we moved next door. The mothers had regular meetings in which Lil offered reports of what she had seen from her kitchen window. They compared notes and considered what to pass along to the working fathers. We called them "The Mom Squad." Lil lived with the hope that she could raise an honest and respectful son. Ruth and my mom prayed only that Dave and I wouldn't burn down or blow up one of our houses.

"They hit the baseball right at my window," Lil complained.

"They should bike to the park," Ruth offered.

"Too far," Lil argued.

"They can bike four blocks to the school," my mom suggested.

"They play in the middle of the street."

"The cars are going too fast."

"How do we know whose boys will be down at that school?"

"They don't watch for cars when they ride their bikes."

It went on like that every Saturday morning at one of their Formica kitchen tables.

Our dads had different issues.

Morry Weinberg worked at a plumbing supply place. He bought the first television in our neighborhood at least two years before anyone else. It had a ten-inch green screen with a big magnifier attached to the front. Every evening, Morry sat in the room he had built by enclosing the breezeway between his house and detached garage. He did all the framing, paneling and trim without the benefit of power tools. After we moved in across the street, my dad met Morry as he held the final finishing nail between his forefinger and thumb.

"Hello! I'm Sherman. I live across the street," my father said.

"Hello. I should have come over when you moved in a couple of weeks ago. I feel so guilty. But I've been up to my armpits in this new room," Morry explained. "Forgive my rudeness."

"No problem," my dad responded. "I've been on the road the past two weeks. We haven't even opened all our boxes. I heard your hammering and thought I'd offer you the use of my table saw. It's right over there in my garage. Any time you want …"

Morry looked around the room at the fully installed woodwork that he had spent two weeks cutting with a dull hand saw.

"*Now* you tell me," he said.

That started a love between our families that lasted many years. Morry told the saw story at many gatherings. Lil always tried to persuade him not to, but my dad insisted. He loved self-deprecating humor, and the story always ended with laughter all around. Morry told it better every time.

Oscar Anderson, Dave's dad, walked with a heavy limp. All his life, he worked around one leg being ten inches shorter than the other. That didn't stop him from being Mr. Build-It on our block. Oscar reigned as king in his garage. Our whole upbringing, Oscar directed us through soapbox

16

cars, go-carts, sailboats and auto fixer-uppers. He taught Dave and me how to use every tool in his garage. He knew how to plan and implement anything, and he *always* read the directions.

"Wait awhile. Wait awhile!" His favorite expression meant two young boys were progressing way too fast. We hadn't followed the directions to his level of understanding. "Wait awhile." Those words echo softly in my ears. To this day, I'll whisper them to myself when confused with directions. I'll take a breath, say "wait a while" to myself, and continue more deliberately.

As a civil engineer, Oscar saw life as more science than art, and anything we built in his garage came out exactly as the directions indicated. I learned about patience and excellence from him.

Lil's parenting philosophy was to watch and report with the hope that diligent attentiveness might evade calamity. Mom thought we were just normal boys, albeit a bit mischievous. Ruth baked cookies and canned fruit. Morry ignored Dave and I, keeping Steven isolated in clarinet practice several hours a day. My dad's work kept him on the road one or two weeks at a time.

Wonderfully kind Oscar thought the best way to raise energetic and curious boys was to keep us busy. He had a project going at all times. If I came by looking for Dave to join me in some impractical fun, I'd wind up with sandpaper in my hand, rubbing the side of a boat or taking the scratches out of the hood of a junk heap. Oscar gave instructions, read from the manual, kept us moving from one detail to the next, never losing sight of the objective. Through my age of discovery, in the garage next door, Mr. Anderson also taught me about finishing what you start. I enjoyed the confidence that brought.

Dave exceeded me in design and building skills. I played a capable assistant, as he knew how to do most things naturally. Crazy with excitement pulling ropes to steer, Dave and I flew side-by-side in our matching carts down the steepest hill in a nearby neighborhood. We beat those first two carts to death.

Under his dad's tutelage, Dave's engineering talent steadily improved. I thought I'd died and gone to heaven when he learned to weld and made us carts of tubular steel with steering wheels and motors.

While Dave created and built, my early fascination in life was less constructive. I loved burning things. I invented ways, acceptable and not, to watch how things reacted to open flames. In our outdoor brick barbeque, I experimented with all forms of heating, melting, smelting, and blazing. This advanced to explosive projection. Rockets! That's where Dave and I melded. He designed the aerodynamic tube and wings, and I provided the thrust. First, I experimented with the sulfur ends of matches packed into CO_2 tubes. They were remarkably loud and effective, but the rockets blasted away so fast we couldn't follow them. We had no evidence to tell us if they had disintegrated upon ignition or flown to another county. Dave read books about slower exploding rocket fuels. I had no interest in chemistry, but anything that burned attracted me.

Ruth often appeared in the garage to ask us where all the smoke came from. She saw the rocket tubes and launch tower, but she didn't really ask about where our rockets might eventually fly. She only had concern about the massive clouds emanating from a structure so close to her house.

"It's nothing mom. We're experimenting. It's just exhaust."

Shaking her head, she would depart and try to remember to discuss this with Oscar when he came home from work. Somehow, dinner and other priorities usually blocked her short-term memory until Saturday morning. Then, her worries were a welcome subject for the Mom Squad.

Our rocket era lasted a year until a miniature prototype launched itself prematurely on the palm of my right hand, incapacitating me with third degree burns. I missed sports and swimming all summer. We were only nine and ten, and our dads put an end to the rocket boys.

The next weekend, Oscar bought Dave his first boat kit. Every night, they attached pre-cut pieces, and I helped with sanding. Dave and Oscar were the brains of the outfit. I gave only elbow grease. The painstaking process went on for weeks before even the semblance of a boat appeared, but it had Dave's total attention and left me without a companion for other endeavors. I came every evening after supper to offer my assistance.

After school one day, I stood in the Anderson kitchen as David poured two plastic cups with fresh lemonade. He looked over the sink out the window and shrieked. "Fire!" Flames were lapping out from the open garage door. We both ran outside. Dave grabbed the garden hose and pulled it toward the garage.

"Full blast!" he yelled back over his shoulder. "Get the Apathy's!"

I cranked the spigot until it stopped and ran past Dave who aimed the stream at the flames in the garage. I jumped the fence to the house next door, cranked on the water, and dragged their garden hose back over the fence with me.

"Give it to me," Dave demanded. "Call the fire department and come back!"

Like a gunslinger with both pistols firing from his hips, Dave blasted away at the base of the flames with one hose while he wet the half-constructed boat with the other. I scampered back into the house and dialed the number listed on the decal stuck to the kitchen phone.

"2108 Murieta Way!" I shouted. "Fire in the garage!"

I took the second hose from Dave. From a few blocks away we could hear the sirens coming. He had already been effective as white smoke replaced black. The fire trucks arrived within a few minutes and, by the time they got there, there was only smoke. The flames had subsided. The west wall, workbench, roof, and rafters all smoldered white steam as Dave and I continued the water streams pointed at the smokiest places. The rest of the garage and the precious boat remained unharmed.

There were no congratulations. The firemen pulled us out of harm's way and took over with discipline and order. The chief hollered commands and the axes flew through shingles and walls. Fat fire hoses lined the driveway. Dave and I replaced our small garden hoses and met back on the driveway, well away from the garage.

"Benny, go straight home," Mrs. Anderson said behind us.

She had come home from her volunteer job at the church to find three fire engines and twenty neighbors standing in the street talking about the boys who played with explosives.

"David, go to your room and wait for your father."

"But, mom, we …."

"No buts, young man. You go there and wait. I just don't know what I will do with you."

Oh dear.

I left immediately. Dave experienced the highest form of grief. If a mother deferred matters to a father, it spelled disaster. The punishment would certainly be corporal.

I called my mom at her work and told her exactly what happened.

"Sweardagod, Mom. We put it out We didn't start it."

She said she'd be home as soon as possible and hung up without saying goodbye.

Oh dear again.

I could feel the paddle on my butt already as I sat and waited.

Later that evening, after a meeting of the parents that lasted over an hour – a meeting, by the way, that Lil and

Morry Weinberg also attended although Steven wasn't even at home at the time of the fire. Shortly thereafter, my dad returned to lead me across the lawn to the Anderson's garage. He said nothing. Dave and I stood in the area where the fire had left charred wood behind. With the smell still filling the air, our fathers asked us to look around.

"This is the result of a fire," Oscar started.

"Fire is a very dangerous thing," my dad added.

"It could have jumped to the house."

"How many times have we warned you?"

The lecture went on, first one father, then the other, until they were convinced we understood the danger and the damage. Then came the second phase, the part about how happy they were that we were not hurt or killed.

"I don't think either one of you would want to be going to a funeral this week, would you?" Mr. Anderson had the most deadpan scowl I had ever seen on his usually congenial round face. "It is good that you tried to put out the fire, but you should have known better."

Then came the final phase, the "Consequences."

"You boys will not see each other for one month. It is May 21st. You are grounded from each other until June 21st." The sentence came from my dad. He had probably figured out that his son had started the fire in the first place. Oscar stood nodding.

"May I say something?" Dave asked. "Sweardagod, we ..."

"No," Oscar replied. "You may go to your room. You may say nothing. Tomorrow morning at seven o'clock, you can help me clean up this mess."

Our fathers didn't know the Sweardagod oath.

"This is so unfair! You won't even listen to us," Dave cried. His sense of justice destroyed, tears flooded his face.

My dad looked at me as I took a breath to speak. "No," he said, and he led me down their driveway still wet from the hoses, and back across the lawn. Once inside our house, he said to me, "If you see David just once during the next month, there will be no summer camp for you. Now go to your room. Tomorrow we will find some chores for you."

Saturday wasn't fun. My dad had a list for us to do, and we kept at it all day. He felt guilty about not helping Oscar and Dave cleaning their garage, but the restriction took precedence. The two of us worked diligently all day, my father doing his best to discipline his wayward son. I felt righteous indignation. They didn't know, and they didn't want to know. I told my mom the truth and she had undoubtedly kept it to herself rather than suffer teasing at her naïveté by her husband and neighbors.

They were all wrong. I saw my first glimpse of an unfair world. Sometime late in the afternoon, it came to me that I might be experiencing retribution for all the other times I had amused myself with fire-making. God knew all. I had once, in fact, almost burned down the back fence. On several occasions, I had torched autumn leaf piles in other people's sidewalks with a match-shooter I made out of a clothespin. Of course, there was also the rocket fuel disaster.

I ate silently through dinner and made a hasty exit to my bedroom after washing the dishes and putting them all away, a task usually shared with my sister. Given my recent status as a criminal, she got herself excused.

At about eight o'clock, a knocking on my bedroom door interrupted the sad country music sniveling out of my radio. I twisted the knob to off and pined, "Come in."

Oscar appeared first. He limped to my bed and sat on the side. My father followed and stood behind him. I didn't remember Mr. Anderson ever having been in my room.

"Benny, son," he said. "I, well, I guess, we, uh ... this is difficult."

He choked on his words, another historical first.

"We have an apology to make. A very big apology. All of us. To you. To both you and David."

I sat up. What could this be? Oscar moved his hip higher up on my bed to get a better position. He took a giant breath. I searched his face and then my dad's.

"I was wrong," he said.

I looked again at my dad who did not flicker. His lips remained thin and taut.

Oscar continued. "The fire marshal left an hour ago. His investigation concluded that the sunlight, refracting through the tilt of an open window, caused a spontaneous combustion in a pile of oily rags I had left on the floor."

He watched my expression. Filling my head were words like spontaneous, refracting, and combustion. I nodded in semi-understanding. Mr. Anderson took that as an invitation to continue.

"He also said that you and David saved the garage from being destroyed. He commended your first steps in getting water on the fire. You did the right thing in calling the fire department as soon as you had the blaze contained."

These words I understood.

"He said that he always wants people to call right away, but that the garage would have been lost if you had not used the two hoses. The fire might have leapt to the house. Your dad and I are sorry we didn't allow you to tell us what happened," Oscar said. He looked to see if my dad wanted to add anything.

"You are both heroes," came right out of my father's lips.

"We want to make it up to you," added Dave's dad. "Tomorrow, first thing, the four of us will get up early to drive to San Francisco, Candlestick Park. We need to get there by one o'clock to see the Giants play the Dodgers."

The following day, two boys and two dads shared hot dogs, cokes, and baseball followed by a stop at O'Farrell's Ice Cream for hot fudge sundaes. Our dads had as much fun as we did.

Having faced the beast and won, Dave and I gave up our fascination with combustibles. Although they didn't know it, our entire neighborhood became a much safer place. After that, whenever I felt discouraged by my parents' strict rules, I went to the shoebox in the back of my closet and took out the badge that Oscar hung around the button on my pajamas that evening. In thick black ink, he had carefully printed the word "hero" in the middle of a paper star.

Train

After my twelfth birthday, I spent every Saturday with Dave at the downtown YMCA. When summer vacation came, we went on daily field trips. For about fifty cents, our moms could pack us a lunch and get us out of the house for eight hours. They each tried to look concerned as we left, admonishing us to come straight home, but I suspect they danced a victory jig as soon as the door shut behind us. Everybody won.

To avoid traffic, Dave and I rode our bikes on a dirt path that followed the railroad tracks running through town and right past the Y. Our route made a straighter path than the city streets. Most mornings, a freight passed us, slowing as it approached downtown. When we could hear it coming, we'd put pennies on the track and run to hide. After the train passed, we'd look all over to find what the powerful wheels had done to squash the copper.

One morning, the train seemed to be moving slower than usual.

"It goes right by the Y," I shouted. "It's going slow enough to catch."

"No way," Dave argued. "What about our bikes?"

"Not today. But some day."

"I don't know, man."

"They always slow to a crawl when they go through the town," I offered. "It's the law."

Okay, I might have made up the part about the law but he had no argument. We watched many trains passing right behind the YMCA on their way through Sacramento. By the time they got into downtown, they were literally crawling. By Friday, we had dared each other into leaving our bikes behind.

"We'll take the bus home," I said. "Today is the day!"

We ran all the way to the tracks and waited impatiently for the train to come. We weren't disappointed. Ears to steel, we felt the rail vibrating.

"Do you think it's coming our way?" I asked, jerking my head up.

"No, stupid. It's getting louder going the *other* way!"

We both ran to hide behind a fence, out of view of the operator with whom we usually shared waves. As the giant engine came into view, we peeked to see it slowing to a speed we could easily match with our young legs. The cars passed, most of them closed. Finally, a string of open doors came into view.

"Let's go!" I hollered.

"Let's go!" Dave repeated louder, with soprano enthusiasm.

With a few strides and a long leap, we both grabbed the moving car floor and rolled inside. We slapped each other profusely. He hooted and I hooted back. Nobody could hear us. Trains are very loud. For a few blocks, we exchanged comments about how brave we were. How unbelievably enterprising, riding free. We discussed hobos, and Dave told me of tough train guys with hammers who pounded tramps in the skull before ejecting them. He assured me that nobody would hit a couple of young boys, but I stayed back from the door anyway.

"If somebody catches us, just jump and keep running. No way they chase us and let the train move away from them." He made me feel a bit better about the hammers.

The inside of a freight car is bare unfinished wood on all sides, top and bottom. It's just a big rectangular box with a sliding door. There isn't a whole lot to do in an empty

26

freight car. We sat and stared out the door. Houses passed. A crossing bell came and went. More houses. More crossings. We were bored. We cupped our hands on our ears, off and on rapidly, and played this echo game for awhile.

Something blew into my eye and it stung. I rubbed it and made it hurt even more. Both my eyes watered. I realized I couldn't open them without the stinging increasing.

"Your eyes hurting?" David asked.

"Yes," I shouted, over the roar of the train wheels. "Both eyes. It's awful."

"Shoot!" Dave screamed. "It's hay! This car carried hay."

The dust swirled and the bits of hay attacked us like locusts. Neither of us could see. I pulled out the tail of my t-shirt to try to clear my eyes.

"Gotta get into another car," Dave suggested, louder than before.

"I can't see where I'm going," I yelled in his ear. "Too dangerous."

"The train is speeding up!" Dave yelled. "That's why the dust is blowing."

"No!" I protested.

I opened my eyes just long enough to see houses flashing by. Both eyes felt like a million pin pricks. I pulled my t-shirt up over my head.

"Help me close the door!" Dave hollered.

"Don't go near the edge!" I yelled, not seeing where he had moved. "Come back!"

Between blinks, I could see him kneeling in the open doorway, pulling at the door.

"Help me! Gotta get this door closed. Stop the wind."

I slipped in beside him and felt the fresh air blowing past.

"It won't move!"

The sound of the steel wheels screeching along the rails sliced through our ears. The creaking of the heavy cars against their suspension added to the dissonance of a dreadful fate waiting inches away.

The door wouldn't budge. We retreated to a corner of the car where we huddled, shirts over our faces, crying in each other's arms.

"Please, make it stop!" I pleaded. "Do something, David. Please!"

"Please, God!" David prayed aloud. "Stop this train now. I promise I'll be good. Both of us promise. Right, Benj?"

"Right," I echoed. "I promise with all my heart."

"I'll never steal candy bars from Consumers Grocery," he said.

"You what?" I asked incredulously, not believing what I heard.

"I'll never pee on my mom's rose bed again," he continued. "Make the train stop and I'll go to bed when my mom asks. I promise. I'll mow the lawn without complaining. I'll make my bed every morning."

I tried to think of something to bargain with, but I didn't have that kind of relationship with the Almighty. I felt glad I went to the Disciples of Christ and wasn't a Methodist like Dave. No way I'd make my bed every morning.

The siren of the wheels increased, clacking against the railroad ties in their staccato rhythm, faster and faster. The dust choked our throats and clogged our noses. My chest heaved. My eyes felt like they were bleeding. I grabbed Dave as hard as I could and, with my face buried against his chest, begged for mercy.

"I confess everything," David screamed. "You better do the same before we both die, or you'll be going to *you-know-where*."

Fear won. We were only boys, so we weren't much to master. Our bones froze. Our bravado expired into a duet of moans from two defeated victims of their own misguided adventurism. Dave and I experienced a humbling that we never discussed again. Powerless, terrified, and of no help to each other, we pressed our hands to our faces and gave up. We stopped crying, stopped hollering at each other for help, and just curled into a single human ball of misery propped against each others' body for moral support. The speeding train, with its two uninvited whimpering riders, left our hometown behind. I remember humming to myself as it seemed to ease the shrill sounds in my ears. After an eternity of noise and fear, with my eyes shut tight against the swirling dust and hay, I spiraled backwards into the escape of sleep.

"Wake up," Dave said in my ear. "We've stopped."

Disoriented at first, I didn't understand what prodded me, sticking me in the ribs. I pushed his fingers away and rubbed my eyes. The wheels, tracks, creaking cars, and whistling wind had all subsided. I had no concept of time or direction. The quiet shrouded me in an eerie veil.

"Wake up, Benj. We're safe."

Dave's voice sounded calm and authoritative. My first conscious thoughts were that we were home and safe. Then the smell of the dusty wood interior reminded me of losing consciousness in a run-away train.

Together, we crawled to the door and peaked out. Sunshine and sagebrush greeted our bleary eyes. An open field ran to the horizon without interruption. The hay had settled. The stinging had subsided. I felt drained but eager to get out.

"Let's go," I said, leaping from the door.

"Wait!" Dave cried, but he followed right behind me. We looked right and left and saw nothing. Peering under the train, I saw a line of buildings.

"Come on," I said. "Let's get to the other side."

I stooped to crawl through the space between the wheels.

"Are you crazy?" Dave shouted. "What if the train starts up again?"

I looked back at him. He had dark brown streaks from his eyes to his jaw line where dust had mixed with his tears. I realized that I must look the same.

"Clean your face," I said. I licked my palms, rubbed my cheeks, and wiped them with my t-shirt. "It'll take this train five seconds to go an inch. We can out-run any stopped train even if we're crawling."

"Right," Dave answered, as he crept under the train behind me.

It felt great having Dave following my lead for the first time in our lives. He didn't argue a bit. Something had changed in the dust and noise. Once safely on the other side of the boxcar, he took a moment to do as I had done, wiping his face. I pointed out a couple of streaks he missed and he reciprocated. I pulled my fingers through my crew cut, and a pound of dust blew off my head. Dave laughed and did the same. We were a mess. He swept the hair out of his eyes exactly as he had a thousand times, but his eyes had a different look than I remembered. They might have been waiting for me to say something.

"What?" he asked.

"Nothing," I said. "Let's go."

The yard looked deserted. We walked over several tracks, turning our heads left and right at every crossing. We hopped to the pavement in front of a long warehouse.

"Look!" Dave pointed at a sign on the building. "Bowman and Long!"

A furniture store by that same name sat at the end of our street in Sacramento. Something about seeing a familiar store logo reminded us that we did have a safe home, and we might see it again one day. We went slowly along the backside of the warehouse around the corner under the sign.

30

I feared that at any minute some adult would pounce on us for trespassing. On the other side of the building, we saw delivery vehicles backed into garage stalls with "Bowman and Long" printed on the side of each trailer. We walked past a line of trucks with empty cabs. There was no opening to the building not blocked by the rear of a truck.

"Hey, you kids. Whatcha doin'?" a man yelled behind us. We jumped out of our skins. A driver leaned out the window of his truck. "Come over here!" he demanded.

We walked slowly. Dave, the oldest, stepped forward.

"Well, to b-be honest, sir," he stammered, "We just came in on that train back there."

Oh, great! I thought. Why is he starting right off with the truth? This is trouble. I took a breath to speak but couldn't come up with anything that dismissed or even redirected what my partner had confessed.

"You did?" the driver shot back. "You ain't lyin'?"

"No, sir. It's true," I added.

"How old are you two punks anyway?" he asked.

"Twelve," I offered.

"Thirteen," Dave said, thumbing his chest. "And, twelve," he added, pointing toward me.

"Where y'all from?"

"We live in Sacramento, south of town, by the airport," I explained. "We caught the train to go to the YMCA, but it went faster instead of slowing down like it usually does. We couldn't get off."

"Man oh man!" the driver laughed. "You guys got a lot of guts."

"Well, maybe," I said. "But now we gotta get home."

"You look like you could use a long bath and a scrub brush," he observed. I looked down at my filthy white t-shirt and jeans.

"Where are we?" Dave asked.

"Rocklin," he said. "Bowman and Long plant."

"Rocklin?" we both responded.

We had traveled about thirty miles east of Sacramento although the whole trip probably took less than an hour.

"Say again where you live in Sacramento?" he asked.

"Right down the street from the Bowman and Long store," Dave answered.

"On Murieta Way?" he asked.

"Yes, sir," we both nodded.

"Well, I'll be danged. That's exactly where I'm headed. Come on, hop in!"

We climbed up into the cab and Dave immediately started into the story about us going blind and crying in the train. Ashamed of our "hour of despair," I kept very still. It always amazed me how Dave could move past hard times and seem to make the best of them while I was still moping

The driver countered with the time he made a raft and sailed down the Allegheny River with his childhood buddy. They called each other Huck and Tom, but they only ended up far away with no way home and scared to death.

"Didn't run into 'Sam the Truck Driver' going our way," he chuckled.

In the back of his cab, someone had forgotten something smelly. Fortunately, we rode with the windows open. Dave sat in the middle, being the braver of us two. I hung my head out, exhausted in the warm summer air. When I felt drool slithering back to my right ear, I woke with a jerk. Dave was engulfed in stories of a beautiful river in Western Pennsylvania.

"When we got to the Kinzua Dam, we portaged around the big ol' reservoir and down the mountain to pick up the river again at the bottom," he said. "In all, we had to carry that dumb raft around eight locks and dams. What a pain in the patoot!"

Sam offered us hanks of beef jerky and changed the subject. "We truck drivers are just leftover cowboys," he explained, "Or, at least, they are our natural ancestors." I noticed his boots under his western pant cuffs. "Cowboys became horse handlers. They drove the wagon trains and stagecoaches. They drove the teams. Get it?"

"What?" we both asked at once.

"Teamsters?"

"Huh?"

"Teamsters. Truck drivers. They drove the teams, now we drive the trucks."

He glanced over at our blank faces. We had zero experience with skilled workers. I'd never heard the term teamster before. Without a pause, Sam went back to his story.

"The river joins the Monongahela at Pittsburgh to form the Ohio River. At Cairo, the Ohio joins the mighty Mississippi."

"You sailed the Mississippi?" Dave asked.

"Naw. A thousand miles down the Ohio? That'd take months! I'd like to lie to ya and say we did, but when we saw that monster Ohio, we beached the boat and headed home, hungry, and darn tired of floatin' all day."

"And no Sam to rescue you?"

"Nope. Got lucky hitchin' a few times. Stood with our thumbs collecting sunshine for more hours than I wanna remember. Really made me respect the poor old road warrior."

"Well, we sure respect the poor old train hobos," I offered. "That wasn't fun at all."

Dave elbowed me. He hated to admit defeat of any kind. I had a sinking feeling that we two boys would soon be building a raft on the banks of the Sacramento River.

Sam stopped and bought us each giant chocolate milkshakes. In less than an hour, Dave and I were whistling down the long block to our homes with a new swagger.

"We keep this a secret," Dave demanded.

"Yep," I agreed.

"Sweardagod?"

"Swear... da... god!"

Balloon

"What're you building this time?" I asked Dave, seeing a mysterious tube anchored into the shop vice on his dad's workbench.

"A valve," he said.

"Valve? Like a water faucet?"

"No," he answered indignantly. "That would be a spigot!"

I waited. Experience taught me that he'd want to show off at the right time in a flourish of scientific explanations. I had peeked in the pot while the stew boiled. He hated that. After school the next day, on our way home Dave opened the subject.

"Every man wants to fly," he said. "From the beginning of time, man has jumped off things with manmade wings to try to copy the birds. When we were flying kites last fall, you had a stupid idea, but it got me wondering."

"I did? What stupid idea?"

"The gigantic kite, remember?"

I remembered. We were lying flat on our backs watching our two kites soaring above us, slowly curling left and right in the slightly variable wind. Each had the benefit of three balls of five-hundred-foot string. They were dots in the sky. I suggested that if we made a kite big enough and had twine strong enough, one of us could be strapped to it and soar above the houses and trees. I didn't intend it as a realistic option. Our minds were floating with the clouds.

"I studied the aerodynamics and the wind-to-weight ratios," Dave continued. "I weigh about 130. To get me airborne, and handle the pull and the sudden jerks, it would take a steady eighty mile-per-hour wind, a seventy foot wide kite, and a wire with a rating of two thousand pounds."

"But you only weigh ..."

"It has to do with physics of flight," he cut in. Dave knew how to shut me up. Just mention science. He didn't want to talk about the unrealistic as he prepared me for participation in his garage project. "You know that tube in my garage?"

"Uh huh."

"It's a spring-loaded, gas-release valve. It fits in the end of a balloon and lets the gas out gradually when I pull on a string attached to the end."

"The gas? What gas?"

"I have tested it with water. I hooked it up to the hose and it doesn't leak a bit, lets the water out slowly, cuts it off when I let the spring retract. And, water pressure is way heavier than helium."

"Helium?"

"Light gas, like in party balloons."

David explained how much helium it would take to fill a balloon big enough to lift two hundred and fifty pounds, our weights together plus the carrier basket and some added ballast.

"About two and a half hundred-gallon tanks," he had estimated.

"Where do you buy a helium balloon that big?" I asked.

"You ever see that guy standing beside the fifteen foot weather balloon in Popular Mechanics?"

"Yes."

Any kid who had ever waited in the barbershop had seen the weather balloon in Popular Mechanics.

"Well, it has the size and volume to fly us both," he smiled broadly and slugged me in the shoulder. "Right under that picture is a parachute ad. The parachute is thirty feet wide."

I nodded.

"We tie the parachute lines to a basket big enough for the two of us, fill the balloon under the parachute, and off we go."

His smile broadened. He flexed to sock me again, I dodged, but he got me with his other fist.

"Ow!" I squealed. "You're nuts. How're you gonna come down?"

"Easy. But, first, how are *we* going to go up?"

Dave explained that he had calculated all the weights and determined exactly how much gas he needed to lift the balloon.

"How did you do that?" I asked, understanding nothing about the engineering that always occupied his head.

"Well, I'd like to say I used physics, but I didn't. I just measured the volume of a regular balloon, and added weight to the string until it suspended itself in air. Once I had the formula, I divided the weight into our combined weights and multiplied that number by the volume in the balloon. We can blow enough helium into one of those fifteen-foot weather balloons. It's just math, Benj."

"How do you get a balloon and a parachute?" I asked.

"Mail order from the magazine. Ten bucks each. They arrived last week."

"No way! You are not serious!"

"Dead serious, partner. Lawn-mowing money. And, I'm going to order the gas to be delivered as soon as I rig the basket. I need all your unmatched socks."

"Huh? What for?"

"Ballast. I have fourteen spare socks that I'll fill with sand. I need at least six more to add to our combined weights in order to counter the weight of the gas. When the balloon is balanced with both of us and the socks, we'll just hover. When we pour sand out of a sock, we'll gradually rise. When we pull the string on the valve to let a little gas escape, we'll slowly descend. We can't do that forever, we'll run out of either sand or gas, but it'll give us a short flight."

"You can't order helium gas."

"Sure. I just call a supply place and tell them to deliver to my house. Three bottles of helium. They'll do it."

"Who is going to give helium to a thirteen-year-old boy?"

"They will if I say I'm my dad. I can do his voice."

"Holy smoke!"

"Holy Flight!"

Dave looked at me right in the eye. He searched me to see if I would be jumping in the basket with him. Then he looked up into the sky overhead. I could almost see the white silk scarf flying from his neck.

"Let me see the balloon," I asked.

"It's hidden in the garage loft," he said. We can see it right now before my mom gets home."

As we arrived at his driveway, I followed him into the garage where he brought out the balloon, the parachute, the socks, and the basket. He showed me the valve and how it fit into the balloon. I looked at the basket and could see that two of us would never fit in the tiny space together. It had high walls but only enough floor for one small boy. Even Dave alone would be a tight fit.

"Let's see if we can fit in there together," I suggested.

Dave stepped in and motioned for me to follow. We stood side by side with little room to wiggle.

"Won't we want to sit down?" I asked.

My observation had been correct. Dave stepped out and said, "Well only one Wright Brother got to take the first flight at Kitty Hawk. I'll go up, then you can go next."

This sounded a lot better to me. Let him. I could always beg off later, telling him in the hospital that I didn't want to end up in a full body cast like he had.

"This means less gas or more socks."

On Wednesday, when Mrs. Anderson regularly volunteered at the church, the gas truck pulled into Dave's driveway and rolled off three tanks of helium. The driver tied each securely to the fence posts beside the garage.

"Don't untie them until your dad is here," the driver instructed."

Dave and I knew the danger of gas bottles. Our junior high shop teacher warned us not to ever unchain the tanks. He told every class the story about how one dropped, the head broke off, and the rocket blew through the cinder block classroom wall and shot spinning clear across the playground. He made that story up, as did every shop teacher.

The Anderson's detached garage sat at the end of a driveway that ran along the side of their house. A tall fence gate blocked the driveway.

The first thing Dave did was untie one of the tanks. I held my breath as he rolled it across into place. He set up his basket, balloon, and parachute in the square slab of concrete right in front of the garage, behind the gates, out of sight of the street. I sat on his back porch and watched. He didn't ask for any help until the balloon expanded.

"Hold the parachute out," he instructed. "We need to be sure the balloon stays inside the chute until I have a chance to tie it in place.

I didn't like any of this. My stomach flipped as the weather balloon bulged and grew, pressing against the inside of the nylon parachute. I felt it rise off the ground and thought I'd better make up an excuse to go home pretty soon.

"Getting it! Getting it!" Dave hollered.

He grew in confidence as I shrank in mine. I could only think how happy it felt not to be part of this maiden voyage.

"OK. Let's hold it right there," he said. "Gotta tie it off."

The parachute had some form now, swaying back and forth. Dave took four prepared lines and secured the basket to the fence, the garage, and the house. He switched the hose between tanks and returned to filling the balloon. As instructed, I tied sand socks along the inside of the basket while Dave removed the gas hose and inserted his release valve to the balloon.

"Hurry," Dave called out. "My mom comes home in a half hour."

It went quicker now. When the second tank ran out, Dave moved to the third.

"We're there!" he said, but when he crawled into the basket, it abruptly sat back on the driveway.

"Shoot! More gas!"

His calculations were obviously flawed. He took off the valve and filled more gas into the balloon. To me, it began to look dangerously full.

"Is it beginning to lose its shape?" I asked.

"That's normal," Dave assured me as if he'd done this a hundred times.

"How do you know what's normal?"

He kept the gas running and the balloon kept increasing in size. I backed up to the gates. It looked like any second, the whole thing would explode. Just as he once again removed the hose and replaced the valve, his mom's tires hit the front drive.

"David! Your mom!"

"She's early! Untie the ropes," he yelled, leaping into the basket.

Over the gate, I could see Mrs. Anderson collecting her purse and books from the front seat. I froze. The whole parachute and balloon now loomed above the gates.

"Untie them now!" he shouted louder.

David held onto the sides. The basket, even with him in it, now hovered above the driveway, straining against its tethers. I sensed something terribly wrong. Seeing that I

40

couldn't move, Dave untied slipknots from his end. After the third one, the basket tilted sideways and almost threw him out onto the pavement. He hung on sideways and loosened the final knot.

The parachute balloon shot up in a hurry, throwing Dave to the bottom of the basket and out of sight. Mrs. Anderson, casually walking up her driveway to open the gates, looked up and saw a monstrous shape lurching out of her back yard.

"David? Is that you?" she gasped in horror. "David? Come down here right now!"

I ran across their backyard, scaled the fence in a single bound, and flipped over hitting the ground running in my own backyard. As I reached my patio, I leaped up the side of an external fireplace chimney, and onto my roof. I searched the sky above the trees and saw the balloon. It drifted south, now about three inches wide in my vision. I watched it as long as I could, then lost it somewhere over the airport.

Yes, we lived two blocks from the Sacramento Municipal Airport. On that hapless day, the wind blew from the northeast, sending David and his experiment directly over the wide expanse of the airport property.

In about two minutes, I heard sirens. They didn't die out for a half hour.

Landing craft were re-routed. The airport shut down completely in a state of emergency. Airport fire trucks and maintenance trucks tracked the balloon which had ascended, but moved across the property at a slow five miles per hour. Half way into the open landscape, Dave managed to bring his face up over the side of the basket. A bewildered boy filled the binocular lenses of an air traffic controller in the tower.

"Don't shoot," he hollered into his police-band radio. "There's someone inside that thing!"

The ground crew put away their rabbit rifles and went to their vehicles to chase the flight as far as the south border of the airport. At that point, the city police, two fire trucks and an ambulance took up pursuit.

Dave had no control. His valve stuck the first time he tried to let out pressure to descend, and the balloon continued to rise. One hundred, two hundred, three hundred feet. He had attached the basket using the lines that came with the parachute, but this was one of several faulty calculations. The ropes were too long compared to the width of the filled balloon.

Figure 1 shows the relationship of a normal hot-air balloon shape to the carrier basket below.

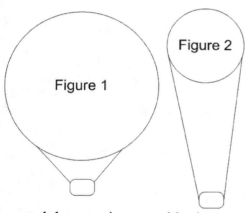

Figure 2

Figure 1

Figure 2 shows Dave's ratio, not very good for stability.

The balloon swayed significantly. The sudden thrust upward threw Dave from his knees to his back and the combination of the speedy elevation with the sweeping pendulum motion gave him instant nausea.

"Straight up in no time," he explained later. "I felt like a yoyo swinging freely, stomach flipping every which way."

Grabbing again for the string to exhaust some gas and bring the balloon down, Dave pulled too hard on the stuck valve and snapped it off at the stem, leaving it useless. His stomach got worse. After briefly looking down, he laid back, held on, and rode out his adventure with only the balloon and parachute above him in view. He didn't look over the side again. He had no idea how high he had lifted or in what direction he traveled.

Meanwhile, the police and fire chase teams came to the end of city streets. The only country roads leading south took them too far away to track the flight. Dave had slowly outrun them and now headed south across the expansive agricultural farms that spanned the valley between Sacramento and Lodi. The city police called the county sheriff, but he had no off-road vehicles. He suggested that they call the police training academy located within a mile or so of Dave's trajectory. The call went out and a group of cadets jumped onto street bikes and headed off across the farms in the direction of the boy in the balloon.

Re-routing around irrigation ditches and fences, the academy motorcycles didn't make up much ground on the drifting balloon. After over an hour and about six miles, the balloon eventually lost enough pressure to begin its descent. By this time, Dave had passed out. He became so sick, he fainted. Two of the motorcycles managed to stay within sight and they were there seconds after the flight ended with a bump, another bump, and a soft crash against a cattle fence. The policemen reported that their victim appeared unhurt, however covered in vomit, and was coming home on one of their bikes. They punctured the balloon and stacked the rubble of the craft into a pile.

Dave spent the evening at an emergency room in observation for internal injuries, but he walked away unscratched. They took a series of tests because he may have hit his head when he landed, and his parents took the opportunity to "have his head examined" for other reasons. Dave said the bearded doctor asked him to follow a pencil with his eyes without moving his head and asked him a hundred questions about his general happiness.

Once again, my parents grounded me from seeing Dave for a week. That didn't stop us. On the night after the flight, we met each other in the dark after everyone had gone to sleep and rode our bikes through acres of farmlands looking in the moonlight for the wreckage. We weren't successful. After several late-night trips, we gave up the search.

Neighborhood kitchen tables reverberated with melodramatic moaning of "ain't it awful," but nobody spoke a word to us. Dave's dad might have felt responsible because he had lent some advice concerning the valve construction without inquiring about its intended use. Being an ever-forgiving soul, he laid it off to a lesson he had neglected to teach his son. A few days after the incident, two men in dark suits with black attaché cases parked in the Anderson's driveway and went inside for over two hours. The car had government plates. I just happened to be riding by on my bike, several times. Still, nobody said anything. My parents never mentioned the balloon flight.

Dave didn't implicate me. He swore he did it all alone and didn't even know my whereabouts. We were back together in a week, planning our next adventure. Sweardagod.

Oops!

Sometimes things just don't go as expected. Somebody told me, "If you want to know if God has a sense of humor, just tell him your plans." I like that. I mean, if God can have a sense of humor, I suppose I should too.

The trick is to stay open to outcomes, not attached to them. No matter how badly you goof up, this too shall pass.

Beads

Coveting the green bead door-curtain to my friend Roger's bedroom, I wanted to make one of my own. When I asked where he got it, he said, "My mom dyed macaroni, and I strung twenty-four lines with heavy thread. Each has a hundred pieces. It took forever."

Undeterred, I surveyed the dye boxes at the grocery store. I chose brown so mine would be unique in color at least. I opened a sixteen-ounce bag of macaroni my mother had in the cupboard and counted fifty pieces to a cup. To make two dozen brown strands hanging in my doorway, I came home from the grocery store with two packages of dye and six bags of macaroni.

The kitchen was socially off limits to boys during my upbringing, except for the occasional peanut butter and jelly sandwich. Dying macaroni wasn't exactly preparing a meal, but it did require using pots and the stove. The instructions on the box said to boil water, add the powder, stir it well, and then add the product to be colored. I did exactly as instructed. All six bags!

My mom's largest pot soon ran out of room as the macaroni expanded well beyond its raw size. I poured half the brown contents and boiling water into a second container, spilling some of it on my white Levi jeans. When I returned from throwing the stained jeans in the washing machine, the contents on the stove had doubled again. I had four pots boiling before I discovered the obvious.

The macaroni shouldn't be cooking.

I called Roger, and his mom answered. "No, dear. You must dye them with very cold water and immediately dry them on screens in the sunlight."

Roger had left out an important step in the instructions. I turned off the four burners and drained the cooked contents through a colander in the sink. This took awhile.

My little sister, Janice, came into the kitchen. "WHAT is *THIS?*" she screamed, pointing at a large pile of cooked macaroni steaming off newspapers in the middle of the floor.

"Cooked macaroni," I said with confidence.

"Why is it brown?"

"I dyed it."

"Why?" she asked.

"Quit asking questions and get me a bucket from the garage."

"It looks like really big dog poop," she observed. "Nobody's gonna eat *that!*"

"Just get me a bucket," I said, dropping the last of the lot on the pile.

"Yuk," she said. "I'm getting out of here."

"You will stay right here! Mom left me in charge of you and that means you have to help me."

My sister pushed out her bottom lip, "Mom said nothing about cooking dog poop."

When our mother came home from work, she asked me what I had cooked in the kitchen.

"Cooked?" I asked. "Why?"

"All the counters and the sink are crystal clean. That usually means something."

"I just cleaned up," I offered, looking threateningly at my little sister.

"Look in the *garbage,*" Janice blurted.

The fact that she lived to see another day is a testament to my restraint. Mother looked at us both curiously. She went out the garage door to lift the lid and discover a can filled to the top with an ugly brown mess that was still steaming and seemed to be growing larger.

"Brown macaroni?" she asked.

"Oops."

"Would you like to explain?"

"Not really," I said. "Just an experiment gone wrong."

"I think we'll go out to eat tonight. I've suddenly lost my desire to cook," she said.

"Me too," I agreed.

Smoke

Only another second child can appreciate how hard it is to grow up three years behind a perfect sibling. Add that mine is a girl and I'm not, and that she is beautiful, and really smart, and sang like an opera star at sixteen, and did I mention her being every teacher's pet? Well, she was. Those same teachers were mine three years later, and they saw me as the opposite in all ways.

When she entered the second grade, my big sister's worst fear came to fruition. Her little brother entered the same school. My mom tried to take me to kindergarten the first day, but I insisted that I knew the way myself. We had walked with Kay Lynne since I was two, and I looked forward to walking the six blocks to the elementary school on my own. I stood and screamed on the sidewalk in front of our house, begging my mom to let me go by myself. Exasperated, my mom told her second grader to accompany her little brother to school. Kay Lynne refused, causing another scene on the sidewalk. She bargained, she threatened, she pleaded and, as always, her mother won.

We began the long dreaded death march to school. After the first block, however, she lengthened her stride with legs that were already twice the height of mine. I trotted along behind trying to grab at her illusive hand until I finally gave up and walked to school at my own pace. Each morning thereafter, after we turned the first corner, Kay Lynne stretched her legs and doubled her pace.

I relished the idea of at least superficial independence, although I often looked back to catch my mom dodging behind bushes and parked cars as she monitored my progress.

Kay Lynne would rather curl up in our big leather chair to read a thick book or listen to classical music than run for cheerleader or homecoming queen, each of which she had already won in my book. In her senior year of high school, I entered ninth grade, my final year of junior high. At least she wouldn't have to share a school with me, but her other worst nightmare happened. I joined the high school youth group at church. No long strides would out-distance me now. I stood six inches taller. No age or intelligence advantage would stave off the little brother who everyone already knew to be nothing like his most mature and decent sister. She tried her best to avoid traveling together to and from church, but she had a license and I didn't. She again lost every battle with my parents.

"He's just gross, mom," she pleaded.

"It's only a fifteen minute ride."

"That's an eternity!" she cried.

She sought rides with boyfriends, but my parents weren't about to drive me across town with another car headed in the same direction. Her suitors offered to take little brother along in the back seat. Kay Lynne sat with her arms folded in disgust. I told dirty jokes and made vulgar noises. The more the driver giggled, the more sounds emitted from the back seat. These brief carpools probably damaged my big sister's psyche for life. For that entire year, she spent every Sunday commute in teenage social hell.

Youth group meant more of the same. At church, we were all supposed to at least fake that we were trying to be good. Kay Lynne, of course, didn't have to fool anybody. She didn't use swear words, if she even knew them. She wore dresses and carried a small clutch purse that matched her shoes. Her head didn't have a hair out of place. And, worst of all, she always acted really nice. Everybody loved her, and she never noticed.

Her little brother hung around with a bunch of cronies who looked like fugitives from hot rod movies.

Our first summer church camp together went pretty well. At the large conference center, I made different friends and gave Kay Lynne no reason for embarrassment. I stayed busy climbing, foraging, hiding, chasing, and basically looking for harmless mischief.

At the end of camp, our district elected me vice president. This meant that I would be going to an officer's conference with my sister who served as president of the state council. She quietly simmered, alarmed that her district would elect such a disobedient non-believer.

Two weeks later, mom and dad drove us into the wine country north of Sacramento to a beautiful, secluded church camp. Rustic cabins lined one side of a small creek. On the opposite side, across a romantic arched wooden bridge, stood the dining hall, administration offices, meeting house, and a large two-story group house for first-timers where a couple of adult camp counselors stayed on each floor. The returning officers resided in the non-chaperoned cabins across the stream. The moment I stepped out of the car, the older kids let me know with no little degree of passion where I would stay. The welcoming committee seemed more like a triage of segregationists distinguishing the in-crowd from the unwashed.

I threw my sleeping bag on the bottom bunk under my friend Mike, and we hastily set out to find a secluded place to smoke and rag on our pompous superiors. We made up nicknames for them, like Brother Dan, Sister Anne, Bible Bangin' Bill, Holy Holly, and Mother Not-So-Superior.

The state officers and their adult mentor had planned a non-stop schedule of worship services, meetings, lessons, vespers, crafts, meditations, projects, inspirational walks, and nightly campfires to fill almost every waking hour.

Since we had been elected youth group officers, we were expected to behave like we had been scooped up by The Rapture.

At our first meeting on Sunday evening, barely an hour after checking in, we sat on hard folding chairs and listened to an adult leader with a huge cross hanging from a weighty chain around his neck. Every morning thereafter, he ranted sermons to a captured audience that he imagined were his personal flock, in a youth camp as close as he would ever get to his own parish. Confusing sentences seemed endless, winding around metaphors and similes, misplacing the point in a spiral digression of Biblical passages interlaced somehow with sexual undertones of fertility and debauchery. He knew the raging hormones in the room, feeling them in his own loins. Meanwhile, his wife sat nearby fanning herself in the summer heat, half-smiling with her hand protectively perched on a tummy stuffed with her fifth child in seven years.

I couldn't keep my eyes open. I nodded and drooled through long mornings in a stuffy meeting hall while the tall forest, cool streams and rocky hills beckoned just yards away.

As if the initial boredom didn't drive me nuts enough, after a short break, a youth leader would take the podium to regurgitate in his own words what the old man had just taken two hours to say. This charming fellow I held in high esteem for his rock climbing, Frisbee throwing and diving board expertise. I sat up, hopeful for a little levity or verve, or at least a refreshingly hip approach. He prayed deliberately, looking down at his notes, then stood to the side of the podium ignoring what he had laid out there to read. He drew in his breath, lifted his bushy blonde eyebrows that might have been mistaken for the mantel of a surfer or Olympic swimmer, and he exhaled a forty-minute sermon that came right out of the leader's piety. The seniors swooned. The leader beamed. The young prophet exuded Christian charm.

I churned and squirmed.

"When do we eat? When do we swim?"

"He's sooo cute," someone whispered behind me.

"When does life begin again?" I murmured to myself sinking lower in the slick metal folding chair. None of this related to what I lived in my neighborhood, at school, on the playfield, or even in my church group.

About half way through the week, a click went off in my semi-consciousness. The high school seniors were pretending to be adults. They were all under the pressure of starting college in a few weeks, and they were play-acting "all grown up." The same thing would happen to me. But, naturally, I would try to be a lot cooler.

My sister got through the week without once having to share a meeting or eat at the same table with her little brother. This seemed fine to me. By then, I had her figured for a big snob anyway. I spent my minimal free time exploring with my buddies. Fortunately, the schedule allowed an hour in the heat of the afternoon for swimming and an hour after dinner for silent individual meditation. I looked forward to those two breaks every day. I stayed in the water for the whole hour and, after dinner, I meditated with Mike over a pack of smokes and our unofficial research project of who was the prettiest gal in camp.

On Wednesday night, after a very long evening worship service followed by campfire singing that went until after eleven, I lifted my legs to kick the bunk above.

"Hey, Mike. You awake?"

"*Now* I am, dummy."

"Wanna go out for a smoke?"

"I'm asleep."

My eyes refused to shut. Exhausted but too tired to relax, I knew that even half a cigarette, maybe a couple of puffs, would help me get to sleep. Once Mike's bunk quit moving, I slipped out of my bag and peeked over the top at him. Unconscious.

I crawled to the end of my bunk and looked down the long second floor at twenty other motionless guys and an adult counselor. I pulled on my jeans and shoes, crept between the double lines of bunks, and squeaked down the stairs to the first floor past twenty sleeping girls. I didn't turn to look into their bay, just went straight from the stairwell to the door. Under the light on the porch stood two campers, a guy and a gal, talking, swooning, leaning… taking forever to say goodnight.

"Just kiss her and split, Romeo," I thought.

They stood there frozen in each other's eyes like posed garden statues. I couldn't wait any longer. I tiptoed back inside and upstairs to the boy's bathroom. One of the counselors shaved his face leaning over a sink to get closer to the mirror without his glasses.

"At eleven o'clock?" I asked myself.

I found my bunk and threw my shoes and jeans under it in frustration. The quiet rang in my ears. An open window beside my bed didn't offer much breeze in the hot summer evening. Above me, Mike groaned as he rolled over.

I took out a cigarette and lit it, blowing the smoke out the window. The drifting white plume seemed to hover a bit catching the light from the single bulb on the side of the porch below. I looked out and couldn't see the romantic duo. I exhaled again and the smoke trailed out the window and sat in the air, almost as if it had a mind of its own, waiting there suspended in time. It finally disappeared by itself with no help from even the slightest breeze. Fortunately, none of the smoke came back into the room.

With no recollection of even falling asleep, I awoke groggily to the sound of hollering. "Fire! Everyone out of the building RIGHT NOW!"

People ran by in a panic. I grabbed my jeans and threw both legs in at once. When my feet hit the ground, I felt something bite my right ankle. Leaning to brush it off my leg, I noticed a red ring of embers circling a giant hole in my pant leg near the bottom. I pulled my legs out and attempted to stomp the ring of cinders with my shoe. The glowing wouldn't stop. People passing by were yelling at me to leave the building. I rolled the jeans in a tight ball, starting at the bottoms to smother the fiery pant leg.

The counselors herded everyone toward the stairs. "Everybody out!"

"What is that smell?"

"Where is the fire?"

"Smells like electrical insulation. Probably in the walls."

A thick haze covered the second floor. My denim jeans had been burning for a while, it seems. I pulled on a pair of shorts and a sweatshirt, tucked the jeans under my armpit, and shot down the stairs.

My fellow residents were huddled in small groups. I slipped behind them and ran down a path between cabins. Sleepy campers emerged and walked toward the commotion. Looking around to be sure no one noticed, I slipped under the wooden bridge. I took the jeans from under my arm, unearthed two large rocks on the bottom of the stream, stuck the rolled jeans into the hole they left, and replaced the rocks.

Sirens approached from miles away. Their wailing filled the valley which brought the remaining campers and counselors out of their cabins. A hook and ladder appeared, throwing up dust, followed by a chief's truck roaring into camp. Volunteer firemen arrived in pick-ups with whirling red lights fastened to their roofs.

Walking slowly back to where the camp population now stood a safe distance from the building, watching the firemen unrolling their hoses, hearing the captain hollering orders into his walkie-talkie, I passed older campers who were already designing a prayer service for the morning to deal with the emotional turmoil.

Someone sang "Nearer My God to Thee."

A few young girls silently wept in each other's arms.

"Why are you crying," I asked.

"We're just so humbly blessed that no one has died in the flames," answered a face streaked with tears. "The Lord has watched over us tonight."

"What flames?" I asked.

"Oh there were flames," one wailed.

"The Lord has protected his flock," another added.

Yeah, right, I thought. He got me out of there with my smoldering jeans without anybody seeing me.

"Bless these firemen," they continued to pray. "Bless their trucks... and their bravery... and their muscles..."

An adult counselor explained, "Firemen have two tools, hoses and axes, and they use them both."

The circle prayed on, "Bless their hoses and their axes..."

We couldn't see inside the group house, but we could hear the crashing and splintering of firemen smashing walls. They destroyed most of the inside of the second floor. Of course, they couldn't find the source of the smoke or the smell. It sat at the bottom of the creek.

"This old building has bad wiring," the fire chief told the camp director. "That's why we're hacking into the walls. Gotta find the source."

The camp director looked sick.

My legs couldn't move one step forward. Everything had happened while I instinctively drowned my jeans. Trying to hide the evidence of my smoking mishap, I had no idea of the ensuing aggressive action. Obviously, an ash from my cigarette fell under the bunk onto my jeans and filled the space with the smell of textile smoke, not a lot different than the smell of burning wire insulation.

News of the event spread across the front page of the local weekly newspaper. The fire marshal, doing his routine inspection following the call, found the wood structure to be sorely delinquent in meeting county building codes for high occupancy buildings. It had only one exit and no fire escape from the second floor. There were no sprinklers, electrical outlets weren't grounded, and the bathroom plugs didn't have safety circuit breakers. They also found a critical case of dry rot in the foundation.

The old dormitory never opened again. For three summers, I returned to camp to find the building still boarded shut. Several years later, the structure was razed.

Visiting the campgrounds twenty years later, a mixture of guilt and curiosity made me prepared to confess everything and leave a large anonymous check. The secret haunted me with a vision of jeans slowly decaying under boulders at the bottom of a stream. I needed to purge. I needed redemption. No matter who owned the camp now, penance needed to be paid.

Trying to get my bearings, I parked my car in the new circle drive in front of the dining hall. I got out and looked around. The stream still ran casually through the middle of the camp, but that was the only thing that hadn't changed. Looking across a renovated bridge, I saw that the old log cabins had been replaced by larger brick ones. The road between them now had pavement and parking areas. A two-story brick building stood on the other side of the bridge right where the old dorm had been. Ivy already spanned its walls. Covered exterior stairwells bordered each end.

A friendly clerk in the administration building said that the director had been there his whole life.

"Since birth," she said. "His daddy ran this camp, and he grew up there on the hill in the director's house where he and his wife live now."

She said that, sure, he'd like to see me.

A young good-looking man of about twenty-five grinned widely when I began my story about the summer I attended a conference and witnessed the mysterious fire in the old group house that no one could find.

He didn't let me finish.

"The Army Corps of Engineers built that old barracks for soldiers who trained here for World War I. My older brother found a loose board, and we had access to our own private fortress. I smoked my first cigarette in there," he laughed. "Oh boy! Think about how dangerous!"

I gulped hard, trying to prepare how I would tell him the rest of the story. He kept talking.

"We had multiple fund-raisers following the closing of that building. We refurbished and rebuilt the whole camp about seven years after the capital campaign began," he explained.

Some mysteries are better left as urban legend. I didn't offer a confession, but left him a generous check instead. He thanked me profusely.

"Geez, Mr. Sherman, we're going to have to *name* something after you!" he laughed.

"How about a big ashtray right in front of that brick building," I suggested.

"Huh?"

"Just kidding. Long story."

"There's no smoking allowed anywhere in the camp."

"Good thing," I said.

Regardless of the money, as I drove away I felt like I had made a difference. It's more evidence of how the Spirit will use us where we are, whether we're conscious of it or not. Even our misdeeds might be the genesis of something good. And, when this story is published, Kay Lynne will know the truth about the fire.

Sweardagod.

Aaphasab

In a single year from 1967 to 1968, the Disneyland
Character Department grew from about a dozen characters
to over eighty. Our out-of-costume personnel increased
from a manager and one leadman to a manager, two
supervisors and eight leads. Given the new faces crowding
our dressing room, those of us who had been around in
earlier times felt the threat of losing our identity. I couldn't
remember everyone's names. At a staff meeting, I suggested
we do something to bring the department together.

"Like what?"

"Like a party for only characters," I offered.

"Nobody will come," one of my fellow leads said.
"We've grown so big. We don't have a tight little group like
we used to have."

"It'll flop," somebody added. "If people can't bring
dates, they won't come."

I thought for a minute while several others agreed that
my idea stunk.

"Come on," I said. "We can be creative."

"What do you suggest?" my manager asked. He seemed
impatient with the time our disagreement took away from
his agenda.

"A pot luck," I said.

"Oh please!" somebody sarcastically fumed. "This isn't
church."

"No wait," I continued. A 'bring your own steak' barbeque. We can get a keg. If we have it at an apartment complex, they have all those barbeque pits outside."

"That might work."

"Will there be a hook?" the manager asked. "Will you have some activity or game to get people there on time and have them stay? I don't mind spending a little department money on a keg and some side dishes, but I don't want people to have a couple of beers and split. I don't think that accomplishes your intention of bringing the department closer together."

"Sure," I said, now inventing as I spoke. "We'll give out awards."

"I like that. Go on. What awards?"

"Uh, funny off-the-wall stuff," I said. "You know, having fun with habits and stuff. Like, the 'Locker Room Lawyer' award for the guy who always gives advice whether he's good at it or not."

"Charlie!" three people said at once.

"And, the 'Band-Aid' award for somebody who gets hurt the most."

"Harris!" somebody shouted.

"No way," rang a rebuttal. "Gotta be Jimmy!"

"Yes, Jimmy," came a second to the motion. Already we were laughing.

"See, it's easy," I said. "And, it'll be all in fun. No embarrassing or insulting awards. Just stuff everybody already knows. We could come up with about fifteen of these in a half hour, if you guys help."

"Sure!"

After some more awards discussion, the party idea became unanimous in agreement. We got the manager's approval and I met once more with the leads to determine the actual awards and their recipients. We decided to give one serious award called the "Character of the Year" to the person who did the best job over a sustained time. We wrote up a little citation as a declaration of what it meant to be a costumed character. Some pride and honor entered the prospect of a fun event.

I bought fifteen plastic Mickey Mouse coin banks from one of the shops in the Park, took them home, and painted fourteen of them silver with glossy spray paint. The last one I painted gold for the one serious award. I bought raw wood plaques from a crafts store, varnished them with a high gloss, and glued the Mickey statues to the wood bases. Finally, I spent about a buck each for engraved plates with the names of the awards and recipients. My total cost came to less than five dollars apiece which my manager happily paid when he saw them all lined up on his desk the day before our picnic.

"These are awesome!" he exclaimed. "How did you ever find these?"

"I made them in my garage. They were plastic banks," I said.

"They're so heavy. They feel like real statuettes, like Oscars."

"I filled them with plaster."

"Huh? How did you ...?"

"Coin banks. They have that big opening in the bottom."

He examined the Mickey in his hand and traced his finger along the coin slot on its back. "Ah, little Mickey piggy banks. You got these in the Park?

"Part of the five bucks," I said.

"Unbelievable," he smiled. "The guys are going to cherish these."

They did. We had a great party. Almost everyone in the department came and we all stayed late. We ate fat steaks and somebody brought about a hundred fresh ears of corn which we cooked right on the fire. After dinner, we announced the Mickey Award recipients. In addition to the

Locker Room Lawyer and the Golden Band Aid, we awarded the following:

- The Mighty Mooch for always borrowing, seldom repaying.
- The Sleepy Award. He'll fall asleep anywhere, in the break area, on the shuttle bus, after lunch, before lunch, even out in the Park in costume once.
- The Bashful Award. He probably won't come up to claim this. He probably is acting like he isn't paying attention.
- The Happy Award. Always smiling. Always has a joke, usually a really bad joke.
- The Grumpy Award. Let's just say he isn't a "morning person" or, for that matter, an afternoon or evening person either.
- The Doc Award. Always has a diagnosis. Always knows some Chinese or Indian remedy. They never work.
- The Sneezy Award. Thank you for sharing the Asian flu with everyone last winter.
- The Dopey Award. What was in those brownies, anyway?
- The Snow White Award for the palest legs in the locker room. He should hand out sunglasses.
- The Pinocchio Award goes to the leading schnozzle, the protruding beak, the abundant snout, and *that's* when he's telling the truth!
- The Big Bad Wolf. Not awarded to anyone who plays the Wolf himself, this is awarded to another character who can get dates without speaking, just by being cute and cuddly. He has received love notes from girls stuck in the mouth of his costume. He had three girls follow him for several hours until he would finally give one of them his phone number which, by the way, he punched out on a pay phone

Great laughter prevailed throughout the mock ceremony. The only complaint, expressed by many, was that we weren't allowed to bring dates. Next year, we agreed, this would be a more formal affair.

Drafted into the Army during the summer of 1968, I missed the next two years in the Character Department. When I returned in summer of '70, the new department manager told me what happened to my idea of giving out a few silly awards at a barbeque.

"This year will be our third annual AAPHASAB," he said. "The last two have been the highlight of our whole year."

"Do we still give out Silver Mickeys?" I asked.

"We sure do. But, we don't make them in our garage," he laughed. "It's such a big deal now, the Mickey statuettes are made at WED by the artists. Last year, we gave out thirty awards."

The department had grown to over a hundred characters since I'd been gone.

"We give several serious awards now. In addition to the Gold Mickey for the Character of the Year, we have Best Lead, Super Supervisor, and Rookie of the Year. We're adding another category this year called Character for Life. It's for somebody outside of the department who has been particularly supportive of our work."

"Wow! This is really big," I said. "How is it all managed? How do you pick thirty awards?"

"It's all very equitable now. We go by nominations. People submit names and descriptive paragraphs. We have a small committee decide what gets on the ballot. Everybody votes by mail from home. It's a big deal and very secret. People who are nominated don't know because their names are left off the ballot they get. What a clerical nightmare! But, the whole surprise element is so important. The supervisors and I pick the serious awards, like the Character of the Year."

"I'm glad you kept that."

"Yes. Still the only gold Mickey,' he answered. "And, we kept the Locker Room Lawyer and Golden Band Aid."

"What about all the dwarf names?"

"Some survived. You'll see. People come up with new ones every year."

"And, we're inviting guests now?"

"Yes, of course. After your first year's success, we opened it up. Last year, two hundred people came.

"Two hundred?" I gasped. "You sure didn't have a potluck barbeque."

"We had the ceremony at the Disneyland Hotel in the banquet room catered at twelve bucks a pop."

"Serious money," I observed.

"We clear enough profit from the banquet to pay for the awards. And we invite honorary guests each year."

"Like who?" I asked.

"Last year, Blair the 16mm Guy and the still photographers all came. The first year, we invited Roy Disney, Jr. and his wife. They came. We were really surprised. He's on the Disney Board now, and he loved the whole thing. It made points for us. Several division heads came when they heard Roy Jr. would be there."

"And, tell me about the name."

"AAPHASAB?"

"Yes. What's that?"

"That won the Name the Event vote the year you left. It means 'Annual Academy of Pageant Helpers Arts and Sciences Awards Banquet'."

"Wow. Who can remember all that?"

"Surprisingly, all the characters. Being able to recite that correctly has become a right of passage for the new guys."

The summer came to a close, and I looked forward to the awards ceremony born in my garage. I wasn't disappointed. The banquet had become a gala affair for people to wear their finest party clothes. The Pageant Helpers I remembered seldom wore anything but t-shirts, cut-offs, and flaps. The five presenters wore tuxedos. One of the supervisors explained the origin of the dress code.

"We have females in costume now. It's a big social adjustment for them to wear a heavy costume and sweat all the time, especially in summer. They wanted to dress up for AAPHASAB. And, wait till you see them. It's worth it to the costume guys to have to wear a coat and tie. The women in this department are all gorgeous!"

The Disneyland Hotel dining room was professionally decorated and a jazz band played during a hosted cocktail hour. You'd find no beer keg at this event. After dinner, we were entertained by a professional comedian in preparation for the big event, the awarding of the Silver Mickeys. We laughed at the inventive barbs aimed at fellow characters, and swelled with pride as our manager read the poetic declaration that preceded the Character of the Year Award. No surprise to the audience, the recipient walked slowly to the podium in his own astonishment and humility.

"He'll never forget this moment," my date whispered in my ear.

After the final award and applause subsided, our manager stood to say that the committee had decided upon one additional award.

"We do not intend for this to be given every year," he explained. "But, we want to recognize someone outside of our department who has supported and worked closely with us for a long time. So, we have established the Honorary Character for Life Award."

A quiet response rumbled across the audience.

"The first award is given to ... drum roll please."

We all thumped on our tables.

"For many years, since opening day in 1955, he has quietly worked, and professionally represented Disneyland. And he has done his special artistic work with the characters as his favorite subjects ... Ladies and gentlemen, the first Character for Life Award goes to the Sixteen Millimeter Man, Mr. Blair Clark!"

The Disneyland Character Department forever found itself joined at the hip with the Public Relations Department. When the call came for a photo shoot, they wanted Mickey, Pluto, Donald Duck or any assortment of other costumed characters. We all jockeyed for position on the call list when we heard about a publicity event because it usually meant meeting celebrity movie stars or politicians, even world leaders. As Goofy, I personally stood between Mikhail Gorbachev and his wife, held hands with Liz Taylor and Peter Lawford, strummed a fake guitar between Buck Owens and Roy Clark, danced with Julie Andrews, and rode the Tea Cups with Elliott Gould and Barbra Streisand.

Life in costume meant continuous exciting interruptions. As the photographers clicked away, they encouraged us to exaggerate our animation to gain spontaneous laughter from our famous guests. We guys in the costumes, professionally called Pageant Helpers, got to know the photographers very well.

Blair Clark, "The Sixteen Millimeter Man," handled moving pictures. He had hundreds of television news credits on his resume. You couldn't miss him. He carried a professional movie camera with a long telephoto lens. He also lugged around his tripod, a battery pack, and a large camera bag, all strapped by slings around both shoulders crisscrossing his back. Blair had a private and quirky nature. He acted independently, apparently more interested in his equipment than his subjects. He constantly fussed with lenses and light meters, switched his apparatus from one gadget to another. Most of us saw him only behind his equipment with one eye in the lens.

One had to have a reservoir of patience when posing for Blair. He mumbled to himself as he looked through the eyepiece then adjusted everything again while we waited for instructions. When it came time to shoot, he'd tell us, "Do what you do," and we'd begin dancing or mugging for the camera.

"Hmmm, maybe I should try a little more light, um, yes. Let's open 'er up a bit here. Let's see." He talked to himself just under the level of clarity.

Clark continually moved the camera so he could get a lower angle from the ground or a higher one from a bench. Sometimes he'd arrive with a stepladder over one shoulder and all his other equipment hanging off his other side.

The still photographers were seldom satisfied with one pose. They'd say, "Chin up, a little left, over, over, that's good. Can't see your left arm. There. Thanks. Now, lean into the camera a bit, a little more, that's right."

We'd follow these instructions as best we could. If you were inside a seven foot bear, you had a limited notion of how far out your backside and head extended. But we worked well together. The still guys gave us a hundred instructions, and they'd say "smile" before shooting, making fun of the fact that we were hidden inside a costume.

The Sixteen Millimeter Man started rolling before any warning when we were interacting with guests or celebrities. He preferred informal shots. He called them "fill material."

At AAPHASAB, Blair received a standing ovation. He looked terribly embarrassed but grateful. Bracing himself to do what he probably hated the most, speak in front of a mass of people, he took his place behind the podium about five feet from the microphone. His camera hung from his right hand, a part of him he never left behind. As we continued to applaud, he raised the camera to his eye and pulled the trigger sending a wide beam of light across the audience. He slowly panned from his right to his left. In his view finder, he saw a throng of friends he didn't even know he had.

"Thank you," Blair said once. We quieted and sat. Knowing him to be soft-spoken, everyone leaned forward. He took a deep breath. "I only do my job, and without you crazy guys I couldn't do it." He paused to check his emotions. "From my heart, I thank you."

Tears streaked every cheek in the room. The honored recipient walked back to his table where he accepted the outstretched hands of his fellow photographers.

The next year's awards will go down as the AAPHASAB no one will ever forget. Everything went as planned, like the years before. The awards were given. An honorary character award went to the head of the Disneyland Security Department who had done much to enhance the characters safety in the park. Blair Clark presented the award reading from a beautiful poem he had written for the occasion.

As we stood to leave, our manager asked for our attention. He had Blair standing next to him. "Um, I almost forgot. We have some last minute dessert."

At his words, the kitchen doors flew open and waiters came running out with something flaming off their trays. In the flurry that followed, we didn't notice the 16mm projector being set up in the middle of the room. Down came an electronic screen. Blair Clark showed more confidence than we'd ever seen.

"I have had a year to reflect upon the wonderful honor you bestowed on me," he said. "While you eat your dessert, I have a treat to share with you."

With that, he nodded at the projector operator. The lights dimmed and Blair's collection of outtakes began. He had prepared twenty minutes of characters playing around backstage and some never seen footage from news shoots. To us, as insiders, they were riotously funny. He showed a series of children punching, kicking and grabbing our tails

70

followed by a more tender collection of other children in long loving embraces intermingled with shots of their parents' faces as they observed their kids' dreams coming true. Then, dramatically changing tempo again, there were break-area shots of sweaty bodies climbing out of steamy costumes following a long hot summer parade. He had footage of characters doing things the public would never see. We watched the infamous "bears series" that Blair had assembled from break area scenes. It showed costumed bears committing assorted acts of grabbing each other in private places, faking the flinging of their own feces at the camera, doing basic bump and grind movements akin to burlesque strippers, and the final atrocity, Br'er Bear trying to mount Baloo from behind. The rudeness and inappropriateness of the clips, by Disney standards, had the audience in stitches.

The film leaped in rapid succession from one scene to another. These bloopers and outtakes were strictly taboo. All of us were taught never to get caught by a camera when we weren't in complete costume. Blair had broken our code.

Snow White sat at a table with a bunch of guys eating ice cream cones. She wore her blouse and wig, but cut-off shorts instead of her dress. She casually applied lotion to her legs. Two of the Three Little Pigs danced a lewd dance. Captain Hook and Peter Pan shared a cigarette. Cinderella sat on the back of her pumpkin carriage reading a fashion magazine with the half-naked bust on its cover in full view. Mickey Mouse came into the break area, took off his head, and placed it on a stump. On film? Pure sacrilege! As the forty-year-old heavily whiskered diminutive man emerged from the cute little mouse head, he saw the camera and made an obscene gesture.

Blair had included an unknown clip of Walt Disney in 1955 at the planter in front of Disneyland, standing with Mickey Mouse, waiting for a professional film crew to shoot opening day ceremonies. Blair had been there, capturing his own version of the historic occasion. We watched as the fatherly figure of Walt Disney got more and more impatient.

"OK?" asked Walt. "Well, then what?"

There came a long uncomfortable pause as our Founder and father of all the characters looked frustratingly at the cameras in front of him. Mickey, at his side, responded the only way he could – with his wide painted-on grin.

"OK, then. Can we do this?

Dead space. A longer pause.

"Well, what are you doing?" Walt shouted. "I've never seen such a bunch of dumb idiots!"

The AAPHASAB audience howled. It went on like this, Disney losing his cool, threatening people, starting to give his speech then being interrupted by somebody behind the camera saying "Cut!" because the light wasn't right, or the film jammed, or they had a sound problem. And, as Walt lost it, there stood Mickey with that same plastic smile.

"Look at Mickey," somebody shouted. "He's oblivious!"

We roared. Poor Walt. He started and stopped, swore at the camera crew, took his spot again, tried and failed, and found more cuss words to describe his worsening emotions. To be fair, this occurred on opening day. Walt probably felt more pressure at that particular moment than ever before in his life. Fortunately, no one from Walt's family or any official from the Disney Studios attended our banquet that year.

Finally, the show came to an end with a film clip that thereafter approached mythical proportion – the "baby carriage" scene.

In front of Sleeping Beauty's Castle entering Fantasyland, Blair set up his 16mm camera for shooting the football teams who were to play against each other in the Rose Bowl. There would be a parade featuring the Disneyland Band, a full host of characters, marching bands from each of the universities, and some politicians and other officials waving from Main Street vehicles. The parade would climax in a few minutes at the front of the castle where the teams would pose for publicity shots.

Blair set up his camera in the Plaza Hub and tested his telephoto lens to be sure he had picked the optimum position to record the event on film. The plaza in front of the castle had been cleared of pedestrians by several security officers who were now directing people to use sidewalks to the right and left sides.

As Blair aimed his camera and ran film through it, the horse drawn streetcar approached from the right and stopped in the middle of his frame. This meant the parade would be arriving soon. Rather than take the big draft horses off the street for a short parade that ended at the castle, the streetcar driver would precede the parade, stop at the castle, and go around the Plaza Hub as the parade entered from the other side. He could then continue back down Main Street and avoid being in the way.

Blair used the stopped streetcar to focus his camera. As he moved the telephoto lens in and out and adjusted the focus, which caused the picture to become bleary then clear several times, out of nowhere a man obliviously pushed a stroller into the scene. The carriage was tilted back into a prone position as the baby napped. The man grabbed his camera and stepped forward to take an unobstructed picture of Sleeping Beauty's Castle.

The court in front of the castle slopes gently away from the drawbridge downward toward the street. The man with the baby obviously didn't comprehend the slope. When he stopped to take the picture, his baby stroller ever-so-slowly eased backward toward the street, directly toward the horse and streetcar. Blair followed the rolling stroller as it backed down, down, down, until it gently dropped off the curb. First the back wheels. Bump. Then the front wheels. Bump.

It came to rest between the horse and the streetcar. Fortunately, it remained upright and didn't hit the horse's hind legs.

Unfortunately, at that very moment, the Clydesdale's tail raised, and out came balls of waste plopping directly down and disappearing into the open baby compartment.

Sweardagod.

The banquet hall first sat still then exploded in screaming hilarity. In the background, from the camera's microphone, we could hear Blair's voice.

"Oh, dear me. Oh no." Blair cried "Oh!" as each plop landed squarely in the stroller.

The horse's tail went down, ceasing the avalanche. At the same moment, the father saw that his baby had rolled away. He ran to the stroller and looked down in horror. Blair zoomed in on the dad's contorted face and froze the frame.

Blackout.

"The End" appeared on the screen.

Half of us were on the floor. Others were standing, shouting, "Show it again. Show it again!"

"Next year, maybe," Blair said rewinding his film, "if you invite me back."

Goal

Chapman College had been my first choice as long as I could remember. My parents were alumni as was my uncle. I knew others who studied there including my older sister, some of her friends, and a bunch of people from summer church camps. It fulfilled all the important elements of how I wished to pursue higher education. Most students lived on campus, and it sounded like one big party. There were cute girls everywhere, a dance every weekend, and a poker game every night.

The other major attraction was a very competitive basketball team. Being a point guard in 1963 should have been all I needed. Only a few college teams had heard of the new system of using one guy to handle the ball while pestering the other team continually in a full-court defense. Alas, a good sports idea spreads like a virus, and by the time it came for me to attract a college coach, every high school had point guards. Most of the guys from my high school team had offers from known universities. Even though no scholarship came my way, I hoped I could "walk-on" to the small college team and find a place on the bench my first year. I knew it would be time-consuming, but classes and studying had not yet entered my vision of college. The prospect of later attaining an athletic scholarship I rationalized as the same thing as having a job. In the months preceding college, I imagined various scenarios of my being discovered as a hidden talent.

On my first day of freshman orientation, a tall black guy named Frank Franklin filled my door. He stood 6'6" and had a basketball stuck under his arm.

"I hear you play some ball," he said before even introducing himself.

"Sure. I guess."

"There's a pick-up game over at the gym. I need a partner. How 'bout it?

This meant that I would be guarding this rather tall person whose friendly demeanor didn't dismiss his lofty frame.

"Uh …"

He threw me the ball

"Let's go."

A guy who is new to the territory automatically surveys his competition. All of the young men on the court were better than the best player I had ever opposed. None were shorter than Frank, and all could dunk. They hit shots from everywhere. They jumped like Southern California had half the gravity of my hometown. My shoes felt like they weighed eighteen pounds each. When I first tried to catch a pass, the ball shot through the wet on my palms. Nobody noticed. In fact, the whole session became one of obscurity. Nothing about me stood out, not my size, or my ability, or my mistakes. I was invisible.

Frank caught me walking dejectedly back to the dorms. "You got some good moves."

"You don't have to be polite, Frank. I can see what I'm up against."

"Well, you'll do OK. It's early yet. Everybody isn't even here yet."

"Oh, that's even better news. Thanks a lot."

"What's the matter?"

"Nothing. I'm just getting a shot of reality. College ball is way better than I thought."

"What did you expect?"

"I hoped for a scholarship… next year maybe. Obviously, there aren't any openings on that team. There's nobody out there I can beat. Maybe I can play on the freshman team, but that doesn't really seem worth the time."

"That *was* the freshman team," Frank said. "The varsity is playing at Cal State Fullerton today."

He punched my arm as if he caught the joke, and that marked my last basketball scrimmage.

My roommate, Muhota Kimotho, came from Kenya. He dribbled a soccer ball as naturally as I handled a baseball or basketball. In the U.S. at the time, soccer confined itself to university campuses that had international student populations. There were no American feeder programs from secondary education. Most of us American kids didn't really understand soccer. Muhota took me on as a project and taught me the fundamentals. I found that many of the same techniques of basketball transferred readily to soccer. For instance, it is very important what players do away from the ball, how they position themselves, how they predict what might happen next. That works in both sports, on both ends of the field or the court. As Muhota taught me to pass and stop the ball, I applied my learning as a point guard. To me, the assist had always been as important as the score.

Muhota and I kicked the ball back and forth across our room, up and down stairs, to and from classes. He invited me to join a hodgepodge of students who played for fun on the Chapman football field. It gave me a good reason to exercise, and knowing students from a dozen foreign countries broadened my perspective of many other things in addition to soccer.

Occasionally, Professor Henry Kemp-Blair played with us. We learned he had been a goalie on the national team of South Africa. A couple of our best players asked, and he agreed to be our coach. He coordinated efforts with our athletic department including registering us as a club sport and arranging a few non-league games with other colleges.

By our second year, we were a non-scholarship varsity sport with a full season. We played fledgling teams like us from Azusa Pacific, BIOLA, Pomona, Pasadena Nazarene, and Claremont as well as powerhouses from Cal State Fullerton, Pepperdine, Westmont, UCLA and UC Santa Barbara. We didn't win a lot of games, but we had a team, a coach, and real uniforms.

I served more as team manager than a player. I still didn't have the natural skills of my international teammates, so I came early to put up the nets and fetch the bag of balls. On our Saturday games, I made sure the coolers were full of water and acted as boss of the first-aid kit. Once in awhile, if we were behind by four or five goals, Henry would send me in for the final few minutes.

I didn't mind. We had players from all over the world with a wonderful unified spirit among us. We had nothing to lose, and we were having fun. I didn't mind being the number one cheerleader. All of my teammates were fine sportsmen who included me in everything. Muhota and another African played fullback. They could kick the ball a mile. Middle Easterners played our middle field. They practiced a controlled game with many passes between them to gain a few yards of advantage. Our front line consisted of five Latin Americans. Two brothers from Guatemala, Mario and Jorge, were outstanding strikers who accounted for 90% of our goals. The Latinos knew only the fast break. They could run like crazy, and they never stopped.

"Loft overhead," Mario insisted. "I score de goal."

Well, in theory. The ball seldom got to our front line.

Our best effort came against UCLA late in our second season. One wonderful day in May, we beat UCLA at both ends of the field. The final score was something like 10 to 4, unheard of in the usually low-scoring game of soccer. Mario and Jorge were out of their heads that day. The stronger Bruins had no one to stop our speed. After the game, their poor goalie looked as rung out as a dish rag. We were ecstatic. We had mortified them badly on their home field.

A memorable moment came in the visitor's locker room following the game. We shared a partition with the opposing team's quarters that was open at the top. We could hear them yelling at each other about their loss so we remained quiet and listened. When Tommy Prothero marched in and started hollering, we couldn't mistake his voice. Somebody on our side stated to laugh and Henry motioned to hush. We listened to the famous coach yell about how they had embarrassed him, their team, and their school.

"Where the hell is Chapman College, anyway?" he screamed. "Do any of you even know?"

We all held our mouths to keep from laughing out loud.

"How could you lose so badly to such a bunch of small town punks from some unknown small college? We have over forty-five thousand students at UCLA. I'm sure I can go out and find eleven guys who want to play soccer better than you. How many students does Chapman have anyway? Do you want to know? No, you don't. You don't want to know. It would make you sick! But, I'll tell you anyway. Nine thousand. Nine stinking thousand! Can you believe that?"

"Nine HUNDRED!" rang out from our side of the partition.

You could hear a pin drop. After a moment, Tommy stomped out of the room and slammed the door. The UCLA side of the locker rooms erupted in laughter. They all came next door to congratulate us. We each went home with a UCLA practice jersey.

"We probably peaked early," Henry sighed.

We had beaten one big school, but another loomed soon after. We approached our final game of the season with unspoken dread. Nobody wanted to confess it, but we were afraid of Santa Barbara. They were undefeated. They represented very serious soccer. They were bigger and stronger than UCLA, and reputably a lot dirtier. We came into our last game with only four wins in our season. Santa Barbara knew we had defeated their only formidable rival the previous weekend. They weren't about to take us lightly and get surprised at the end of their perfect season.

We played them at Chapman, a slim advantage with only a handful of fans in our bleachers. I got to the field early and put up the nets, chalked the goals and sidelines, stuck red flags in the four corners, and filled the coolers with ice and water. By the time the others showed up, I felt like hitting the showers. I had already put in a full day. When the Santa Barbara bus unloaded, I really wanted to go home.

They looked like Vikings. These were not a bunch of the usual international students from Africa, Latin America, Southern Asia and the Middle East. These guys were Eastern Europeans who had been pumping iron since they were toddlers. One blonde giant had hair to the middle of his back and an earring! I had never seen a man with an earring except in the National Geographic.

By halftime, the score miraculously stood at only three to nothing, but we were bruised and broken. Several of our best players sat on the bench, injured by blatant intentional fouls. Unfortunately, even the referees seemed intimidated by Santa Barbara. There were no yellow cards that day. We were on our own.

Not only did they have size and strength over us, they flaunted it. A kick to the shins, a solid hip-check, or a sharp elbow to the ribcage accompanied every steal. Their message clearly said, "Don't mess with me unless you want to feel pain!"

Our backs cleared the ball every time they could, kicking it hard the length of the field or out of bounds. It frustrated Santa Barbara. They'd move the ball down the field and threaten, then the ball would go flying far away. Muhota and our other back were going to have sore feet for a month. It was a solid defense, but it didn't lead to our scoring any goals. It only prevented them from burying us.

"You have carried yourselves like gentlemen today, boys." Henry said, as we stood in a tight circle sucking on orange slices at halftime. "If the second half goes as the first and we lose six to zip, I will be proud of how well you have stood up against extreme odds."

"No, Mister Kemp-Blair," Alec, one of the Persians said. "I want to kick these bum's asses clear back to Santa Barbara!"

"Right," said a few others.

"Well, boys," Kemp-Blair said, "that may be impossible, but I like your spunk."

"We can do it. Sure some of us are hurt, but let's platoon those positions with our bench guys," Alex continued.

"We have been all defense the first half," Muhota added. "It's time to turn this around."

"Fast break, fast break, fast break," Mario added.

"Every chance you have to make a substitution, put in somebody who is fresh," Alec suggested to the coach. "I don't mind sitting for awhile to catch my breath."

"Me too!"

"Yes. All of us!"

"We need to run these big guys into the ground."

"As you say," Henry answered. "I like that. The best defense is a strong offense."

"Pass the ball," Mario offered. "I shoot, shoot, shoot!"

"Agreed," added Alec. "They are big and strong. We are small and light. Let's run 'em till they puke!"

Jorge responded with a few sentences in Spanish. Mario interpreted.

"My brother says, if we lose, at least they go home tired."

That is precisely what happened. Henry freely substituted people more often than typical in soccer, and they each ran like crazy knowing they would be coming out any minute. Our guys made fast break after fast break. Finally, about ten minutes into the second half, the plan worked. The giant hackers from Santa Barbara lost a step or two. We were able to keep the ball away from them. They couldn't hurt us if they couldn't catch us.

Mario scored on an easy pass from the right wing. The big football scoreboard showed Home 1, Visitors 3. The Santa Barbara monsters re-grouped at midfield. They ended their huddle with a unison guttural cheer that sounded primal. They had fire in their eyes.

"Now we pass, pass, pass," Mario told his forwards and mid-fielders. "They are mad. They will chase the ball. Stay apart and pass. Don't worry about scoring. Pass, pass, pass. We'll get them!"

Two yellow flags followed flagrant fouls by the opposing players. The referee warned their coach that the next penalty would cost them a red card and somebody would be sitting on the bench.

"Keep it up, coach, and you'll be playing down a man," the referee warned.

While their coach shouted at his men to get back, run faster on defense, and get their heads back in the game, Mario scored again on the same play two minutes later. Two to three. Our team slammed into overdrive. Santa Barbara totally lost their composure. If they couldn't intimidate and control the ball, they had no game plan. Jorge ran toward the goal, and a Santa Barbara defenseman sent him to the ground with a vicious high kick to his thigh.

Red card! The biggest Santa Barbara defensive back's day ended. We lost our number two striker, but they lost a position on the field. We really liked that rule. A couple of the bench guys and I turned cartwheels.

There weren't any timeouts in those days. At every out-of-bounds break in the action, Henry called to the ref and sent in another rabbit. With the score so close, I ran along the sidelines cheering my buddies along expending almost as much energy as they were. Everyone could feel the momentum of the game shifting. Excitement charged the air.

Jorge limped over to Henry and begged him to go back in the game.

"Yo con Mario," he explained. "Treeks!"

"Treeks?" asked our coach.

"Tricks," I explained. "He and his brother have some moves they haven't shown yet."

"No. He is badly hurt," Henry protested.

"Apparently not badly enough," I said as Jorge limped past both of us, checked in with the referee, and joined the game without Henry's permission.

The miracle he promised ensued almost immediately. Jorge took a pass and moved the ball away from the goal instead of toward it. He limped badly, dribbling with only one foot, as he shuffled the ball toward the opposing goal. The entire Santa Barbara team followed him. They thought he was confused. At exactly the right moment, Jorge leaped in the air and back-kicked the ball over his head, far over everyone's heads. The only player who anticipated this crazy move now ran under the ball as it flew up over the defensive backs. Mario had to sprint to catch the ball. No one stood between Mario and the goalie. He dribbled, faked, the goalie flew in the air, and Mario scored easily. This tied the game at three apiece.

I thought Henry would spontaneously combust. He leaped in the air, flew his hands up and down like a big bird, and picked Jorge up off the ground as he came limping badly off the field.

"Bastante," Jorge said. Enough.

He limped over to the bench and collapsed. I handed him the icepack for his cramping leg, the whistle blew from the field, and the game resumed at midfield.

By this point, the players on both teams were so tired that they were resigned to kicking the ball out of bounds every time someone threatened. With two minutes left, it looked like we would end in a deadlock. Santa Barbara would still be undefeated, but we could enjoy a moral victory if not a literal one.

Another Chapman player came limping off the field injured by a wicked block. Henry looked to his bench and saw what resembled an infirmary. I started to run to the locker rooms to get more ice.

"Sherman, you're in!" he shouted.

Without thinking, I ran onto the field. I ran right back off.

"What position?" I asked my coach.

"Yes. That would help," he said. "Right forward. Jorge's spot."

"Right."

"There's less than a minute left," Henry shouted. "Mario has maybe one chance. If you get it, make a good pass!"

Mario pointed at where I should stand. We were near the goal and waiting for our player to fetch an errant kick. He returned with the ball and deftly tossed it over his head.

Mario screamed, "One-minute play! One-minute play!"

We had no one-minute play that I knew about, but the Santa Barbara players followed Mario closely. When the ball came back to midfield, I stopped it and looked for a place to pass. All defensive players were following Mario running full speed to the left. They panicked thinking Mario had another "treek" developing. I dribbled to my left looking for an outlet to Mario, but there were too many of them, and they were right on him. Nobody guarded me very closely. They could tell I wasn't much of a threat from the forty-yard line.

Mario stopped as if he had hit a wall and headed back to his right, outrunning everyone. He waved at me to loft a pass. He sprinted free of defense. The whole field shifted to follow our striker.

Leaning my body over the ball, I prayed, "Please God, just this once," and I kicked the ball as hard as I could, trying to lead Mario with a perfect pass over his head.

Things don't always work out the way one plans. Instead of making solid contact with the soccer ball, I doffed it. My left foot isn't my strongest anyway, and I really didn't connect with all of the ball. I sort of kicked half of it, with part of my foot, my wrong foot. It went in the opposite direction of where I had intended.

Twenty years of life flashed before my eyes. In suspended animation, my kick flew high in the air and bounced once, twice, three times, twisting with the spin of my errant kick. I could hear people yelling "no" and I knew I had let everyone down. It came to me as slowly as the ball rolled on the ground that it was the Santa Barbara team yelling from the sidelines, not the Chapman team.

The entire field of players, theirs and ours, had followed Mario too far to the right side of the field. Even the goalie abandoned his cage anticipating what miracle might come from our most aggressive player who had scored on him three times in the second half.

My wayward kick hit the middle of the field, nowhere near Mario and those chasing him. After bouncing harmlessly about thirty yards, the ball evaded the outstretched arms of the prone goalie and rolled to a stop one foot over the goal line. It didn't even touch the back net.

The referee threw two hands in the air. Henry mimicked the call and fell flat on his back. In a few moments, before anyone could recover, the referee blew his whistle three times signaling the end of the game.

Chapman 4, Santa Barbara 3. Sweardagod.

Our players screamed wildly. Henry scurried onto the field and hugged every guy, hollering repeatedly that we had won as if he couldn't believe it himself. Santa Barbara walked slowly to their bus without the obligatory congratulations.

Henry found me and shouted gleefully in my face, "That, Mr. Sherman, might be the ugliest goal I have ever seen!"

Beauty is disguised at times. My mom and big sister happened to be at that game, the only one they ever saw me play. They went away thinking I did that sort of thing all the time.

Trudy

Some people are born organized. They are hard-wired to arrange, classify, assemble and dispose. I'm not one of those people. I needed to marry into it. Without my wife's lists, nothing gets done around our house. But, she doesn't even come close to the most organized and equipped person I have every known, Trudy Kowalski, queen of emergency preparedness.

Trudy would insist that she is not obsessive, that her attentiveness is just an effective cover for her rather scrambled ineptitude. We all know better. She's is one fine-tuned compulsive woman. I met Trudy when she trained me as a college admissions counselor. She taught me the importance of counting brochures, maps, applications, catalogs, and all other materials before leaving the college. She had everything but the actual physical campus in her carrying case. When she rolled out her information, a prospective student got the whole picture. Who needed a campus visit? Trudy had the equivalent with her at all times. For long recruiting trips, she filled her car trunk with boxes of college information and put her personal stuff in the back seat. One morning, I helped carry her suitcases from her personal car to the college Pinto.

"Why four bags?" I asked.

Each bag seemed half full, one felt empty.

"I don't want to hurt my back carrying heavy cases," she said. "So I pack a week's clothes in each bag. I use the fourth one as my laundry bag."

In the trunk, I noticed boxes labeled for each week also. She had designated a fourth empty box for leftovers. An envelope of maps sat beside the driver's seat. A pad and pen were attached to the dashboard.

"I don't want surprises," Trudy explained. "I'm a single woman traveling alone. It is important to be prepared."

She stuck envelopes labeled for each week in the glove compartment and locked it after checking it twice. She answered without my asking, "Cash for snacks. I only use my charge card for college expenses. I put a week of cash in each envelope. If I misplace one or get mugged, I won't have lost them all."

My provisions were Hostess Twinkies and Dr Pepper. I wore the same shoes, suit, shirt and tie to all my visits. Seeing new people at new high schools four or five times every day, I didn't need to be fashion conscious. When out of town, I traveled with one paper grocery bag full of clean underwear and a shaving kit. I hung three dress shirts in the back.

Fortunately, Trudy never helped me pack my Pinto. She might have had a stroke.

We admissions counselors tried to end our road trips on a Thursday so we could spend a full day on Friday in the office recovering, assembling paperwork generated by our recruiting, filing out expense reports, calling new schools to schedule visits, and most importantly, sharing our road stories with each other. This final item took most of the day. By virtue of our jobs, we were expressive people, and being on the road alone for awhile left us eager for companionship and laughter.

Except Trudy. She mostly listened.

"Well, I'm sorry, but nothing extraordinary happens to me. I am always prepared, and things go as planned."

That is, until one fateful trip to the San Joaquin Valley. Trudy experienced what became one of my favorite road stories, partly because it's unbelievable yet true, but mostly because it could only have happened to her.

She had been on the road for a couple of weeks. After a full morning of visiting high schools, she drove from Merced to Fresno and arrived late in the day. She checked into a small motel and walked next door to a diner. With a full stomach and a day of driving behind her, she could barely keep her eyes open through the evening news. She dragged herself to the tiny bathroom to wash her face and brush her teeth. She laid out her clothes for the next day on the narrow desk, and put on her nightgown.

"In winter, I always wear my long flannel nightie," Trudy explained.

Too much information. We dared not imagine what our colleague looked like padding around in her red-checkered gown and puffy white slippers. Nightgown notwithstanding, her male counterparts could relate to staying alone in a thin-walled motel that barely muffled the sound of trucks roaring down Hwy 99.

She set her alarm, placed her glasses within easy reach on the bedside table, pulled the bedcovers up to her neck, carefully folded the sheet back against the blanket, and leaned over to twist the switch at the base of the lamp.

Her room wasn't quite filled with darkness.

She flipped the lamp on again, got out of bed and walked over to pull the curtain closed. She got on a chair and stretched each end trying to cover the space that was emitting light. Back in bed, she repeated her routine, flipped off the light again, and closed her eyes satisfied that she had done her best to provide the optimum possible darkness.

Tomorrow, she would visit three schools at eight, nine-thirty and eleven, then drive five hours home. Recalling the hypnotic white lines moving past her car earlier, she fell immediately into deep sleep.

Trudy awakened to a loud crash that sounded like an explosion in her room. In an instant, her bed folded up like an accordion. The foot pushed back to the head. Trudy was sandwiched between the mattress and the headboard. Electrical wires snapped, arced, and shorted in a fiery shower of sparks and lightening blasts.

All went dark again. A truck engine stopped. A door slammed. Heavy footsteps crunched on broken glass. With her legs pressed against her chest, Trudy tried to turn her body sideways, but she couldn't move anything except her right arm. Unhurt, but completely trapped, she flailed her right hand out of the crease in the folded mattress trying to reach for her glasses. She waved her hand and mumbled a faint plaintive cry.

"Hello? Somebody?"

The truck door opened and slammed shut again. Trudy heard the resonance of voices outside her room but could not understand their words. Really needing her glasses, she wriggled to make some room for her body to move, but no dice. She was really stuck.

A delivery truck had backed about twelve feet into Trudy's room, right through the front door and window, leaving the entire motel room blocked. The truck, too, was stuck.

The night manager of the motel showed up rubbing his eyes and asked, "Is anyone in the room?"

Several guests stood outside in their sleepwear. "How would we know? That's why we called you."

He hurried to the office to check the register. Running back in a panic, he leaned down under the truck's front bumper and yelled into the room.

"Miss Kowalski? Are you alright?"

Trudy could not exactly hear the question, but she did hear her name.

"Yes. Trudy Kowalski," she responded.

"You're OK?" he asked louder.

"Good day? Not exactly. Who is there?"

For fear of further damage, the roof collapsing, the electrical wires igniting something, Trudy remained trapped while the fire and police departments deliberated about how to proceed. An ambulance technician crawled on his belly under the truck to the side of Trudy's folded bed. He found her free hand sticking out of the crease in the mattress.

"Hello," he said, shining his flashlight on his own face.

"Hello," Trudy answered. "Are you room service?"

"No, ma'am," he laughed. "Did you order something?"

"Yes. My martini is very late."

They both got the giggles.

"And someone seems to have slightly shifted my bedside table."

"You're killing me," he cried.

"It's only fair. Somebody tried to kill *me* a moment ago. "Where are you hurt?"

"My pride is a shambles. Can you get me out of here?"

"Seriously, are you bleeding? Is anything broken? I can't see you."

"I'm not bleeding," she answered. "And, I don't feel any pain. I guess the mattress saved me. I just want out."

"I had some trouble getting in myself and it doesn't look like you're dressed to be crawling over broken glass. The truck is filling up the whole room."

"We just met and this is hardly the time to share personal secrets," Trudy said. "But, I really need to pee."

"That is understandable. I'm surprised you didn't already."

"OK, no more jokes," she said. "That's making it worse."

"I'm going to crawl back," he said. "I need to report to the crew out there. We'll have you out in a few minutes. Just hold on."

"Um, I won't be going anywhere," she responded dryly.

After someone shut off the power, the medic crawled back to place protective blankets over Trudy and stay with her. On his signal that she was okay, a tow truck eased the truck forward with a long ear-piercing screech.

When the noise ended, Trudy pulled her fingers out of her ears. Her mattress resumed its former shape. She pushed the blankets off and took a deep breath. Several flashlights showed a young lady sitting pertly on the middle of her bed in the center of a demolished motel room. Her rescuer stood up from the floor beside her bed.

Trudy smiled into the light beams and asked, "May I have another room?"

Bonding

Terry and I aren't wilderness buffs. One of the reasons
we have remained best friends is that we agree on
necessities like clean vehicles and always sleeping on a
mattress. But, once a year, the church guys took their trip to
the Methow River for river rafting. I talked Terry into
coming by promising I would fill the back of my minivan
with sleeping comforts and junk food.

"So explain to me again how this tent thing works,"
Terry asked.

"We camp on this high bluff," I explained. "Nights can
get bitter."

"Does the tent protect us at all?"

"Sure. It cuts the wind factor. Of course, I still sleep in
sweats and a wool hat."

"I didn't bring anything like that," he said.

"I brought everything you'll need."

"A bag, too?"

"Yep. I brought you a warm sleeping bag."

"And the tent? You know how to put it up?"

"Quit worrying. I did this last year."

"Once? You did this once?"

"And the year before, and the year before that. I did
five rivers in five days with five guys. I put that dang tent up
and down five times."

"Well, that makes one of us who knows what he's
doing," Terry quipped.

Our river guide lived on a couple of acres as far as he could get from electricity and politicians. His only rules were to use the outhouse and be sure our fires were dead before we retired for the night. On the mountain, our host constantly fought to keep deer away from his vegetable garden, which accounted for most of his food. Our urine attracted the deer, so we had to walk up the hill to his rustic outhouse instead of doing what is instinctual to boys in open spaces. I covered both his rules by peeing on the fire.

As soon as it got cold, Terry and I crawled into our pup tent.

"I bet cowboys just slept in their jeans," I said.

"And that would be why there are no more cowboys," Terry observed. "The perennial rash prevented them from procreating."

My tent mate meticulously arranged his clothes for the next day. He removed his watch and wallet, put his socks into his shoes, and unrolled the sweats I brought for him. He moved way too slowly for me. To avoid certain frostbite, I quickly tossed off my shoes and squirmed out of my jeans. Grabbing my sweatpants, I jammed both feet in at once, arched my back, and kicked my legs forward.

A pair of my wife's silk panties flew out of the leg of my sweats, hit Terry squarely in the chest, and fell daintily onto his lap.

He looked down at the underwear, then up at me. A growing friendship had abruptly been jeopardized. He carefully picked up the panties with his thumbs and forefingers and held them out between us. They were the large kind, the very large kind, the ones my daughters called "granny panties." I don't mean to violate the intimacy of my marriage, but these were undergarments worn in tandem with pantyhose by a woman who had no intention of being in an accident. They looked twice as wide as my wife. Terry peered over the mass of silk and shook his head slowly, as if deeply bewildered.

"Hers," I explained.

"Right," Terry answered.

So much for male bonding. His face said that everything he had ever known about me had suddenly inexplicably changed.

"Sweardagod," I offered, knowing full well that he didn't understand the enormity of that oath.

Still holding the panties in front of him with thumbs and forefingers, his eyes panned from side to side.

"You expect me to believe that your wife, the forty-year-old woman who still looks twenty-four, fits into *these*?"

"Well, I certainly don't wear silk panties," I explained. "They were obviously mixed up in the dryer."

He tossed them onto my lap. "We'll just let this go," he suggested.

"Agreed."

"But, you're in big trouble when I tell her you mixed whites with darks."

Driving

At ten, I covered my bedroom ceiling with magazine cutouts of hot rods. At twelve, I switched them for Triumph TR-3s. When I was thirteen, my parents bought an aqua and white, 1955 Ford convertible with wide sidewall tires, dual glasspipe exhaust, and vinyl tuck and roll upholstery. It was totally cool. It rumbled with a throaty purr of arrogance.

When I turned sixteen, that car was going to be my primary chick magnet, if I could just wait out the months to when I would get a license without exploding with anticipation. Two weeks before my sixteenth birthday, my parents traded it in on an olive drab green, four-door sedan. I didn't fully recover until just a couple of years ago when, at sixty, I bought a Mustang convertible. Friends assume it was a sign of mid-life crisis. No way. The quest for my Mustang started long long ago.

America's history is transported in boats, trains, planes, cars and trucks. Moving freely from one place to another is part of our heritage of liberty. And, nothing says personal freedom like the automobile.

The following are stories from the road.

Erby

Every boy in America sooner or later defines himself atop four spinning wheels. It may begin with a go-cart on the sidewalk, a tractor on a farm, a junk heap that barely makes it down the block, or a hot rod cruising Main Street. One way or another, a guy's got to have wheels.

Chuck Cheshire's heart belonged to stock car racers. His first driving lesson came on a dirt track in Terre Haut, Indiana, where his grandpa put him behind the wheel of a blown-out Chevy and told him to hold tight on the wheel and stomp down on the gas. He slid into the turns, hit over eighty miles per hour twice on the straight-aways, and became hooked for life. Chuck knew cars, all cars, domestic and foreign. Sharing an all-night shift with him, as we both fought boredom, I listened to the history of racing automobiles: Indy Cars, Formula One, off-road, Enduro, Grand Prix, and his first love, stock cars. He spoke with almost spiritual praise for road machines that came off an American assembly line, served a family faithfully for a dozen or more years, then became blessed by the craft of a backyard mechanic who wanted only one thing. Speed.

"Stock cars. Dirt ovals. Summer evenings. Exhaust, dust, burning rubber. Nostril ambrosia." Chuck spoke mostly in short sentences.

Stationed at Tripler Army Hospital up on a hill just outside of Honolulu, we worked graveyard shift 6 p.m. to 6 a.m., twelve hours on and twelve off, two days on, and two off. We were young, single, living in paradise with a three-day weekend every other day. The two guys who worked the other night shift came up with a proposal to share expenses on an apartment two blocks from the beach in Waikiki. Chuck and I jumped at the offer. However, we had a problem with transportation. None of the four of us had a car, and the bus that served Tripler only came about every two hours. Half our days off could be spent just getting back and forth. The apartment idea would have to wait.

Then I found Erby. Or, perhaps, Erby found me.

On my nights off, I played poker with some lifer male nurses who worked on the wards. They played dollar stakes and I usually won a bundle. On a particularly lucrative evening, one of the guys couldn't come up with the cash to pay his thirty-dollar table debt. I bought him out for the registration slips on two cars.

"Neither of them runs," he said. "But you can have 'em if you want 'em."

He didn't know about my buddy Cheshire. The next morning, my car expert inspected the two vehicles sitting side-by-side in the parking lot by the barracks.

"Ain't moved in years," Chuck observed. He crawled under the white Volvo and emerged with a frown. "Rusted junk. Whole underbody useless," he said.

"One down," I sighed.

"Naw, don't be dejected. We can rip stuff off 'er."

He moved over to the baby blue Rambler American, ran his hand under the wheel wells and tapped the exhaust pipe with his knuckle.

"Volvo's got rubber," he said. "This body's better."

Pushing down on each of the fenders, he said the shocks were fine. He opened the hood and leaned in to tug on the belts and check all the wires. He took off the air filter and looked down into the carburetor.

"Looks clean," he repeated. "No battery. Check the Volvo."

"None here either," I said after popping the hood.

It also looked like there were none of the usual wires connecting all the important things that I knew nothing about, but I didn't mention it to Chuck as he had already rejected the Volvo.

"No problem," he assured me. "We can coast start."

Tripler sits high on a hill overlooking Honolulu. A circular drive drops downhill from where we stood to the main road, and climbs up the other side of the grounds, returning to the hospital entrance.

Working in the emergency room and admissions, one of us drove the ambulance when there were calls at night. Week nights were slow. We only had the occasional woman in labor. Fights and accidents happened on weekends when the servicemen hit the bars. We parked the ambulance right next to the Rambler American and kept the CB on so we could respond if called. Being drivers gave us access to the motor pool. We borrowed a jack to change the wheels from the Volvo to the Rambler, and we took a few cans of oil, and a little gasoline to get the car going.

The oil ran straight through the engine onto the parking lot.

"Not good," Chuck observed. He disappeared under the car with a flashlight. "Need tools. Ratchet set. Crescent wrench."

Back at the motor pool, he found a pair of rusted vice grips lying on the ground. He rubbed them with motor oil and they loosened enough to use.

"These will do."

I held the light while Chuck carefully removed over a dozen machine bolts holding an oblong pan under the engine and transmission. The work went slowly as they each had to be very carefully unscrewed not to strip the heads off the small bolts.

"Uncommon size," he explained. "Hard to find. Need them all."

After over an hour, my arm could barely hold the flashlight. The back of my head hated the concrete. How could Chuck continue to work the vice grips? It had to be frustrating and physically demanding, but he had a mental picture of us riding down the highway to our apartment in Waikiki.

"Got it!"

We both crawled out with Chuck pulling the pan behind him. It measured about a foot wide by two feet long and eight to ten inches deep. It weighed a lot more than I expected of an oil pan. He propped it up against the back bumper and directed the flashlight onto a hole bigger than his fist.

"Bad mishap," he said. "Ran over somethin' hard."

Looking at the pan, I asked if it could be fixed. He said we'd take the oil pan to an auto repair shop in Honolulu.

"Can't be too hard." he asked. "Gotta get Erby runnin'."

"Erby?" I asked.

"Yeah. Look."

He pointed the flashlight at the license plate. The letters on the plate were RBY. The Rambler American came with a name.

The next day, we couldn't find anybody with a car who had the day off. We were impatient, so the two of us rode a bus to Honolulu with the damaged oil pan sitting on a bunch of hospital towels laid across our laps. We transferred in Honolulu and took a bus that traveled north through a series of small industrial shops.

"Here!" Chuck hollered, leaping up to grab the cord. "Get off."

We left the bus and lugged the oil pan back a block to an auto body shop.

"Three hundred minimum, plus labor," the guy in paint-stained overalls estimated. "Maybe a lot more. Depends on shipping. There sure ain't one of those on the Rock," he said.

We crossed the street to wait for a bus going back to town. As we sat there dejected, Chuck picked up his head and looked around.

"Smell that?" he asked, sniffing the air like a dog.

"What?"

"Metal burning!"

Chuck jumped up and walked between the houses behind us. I left the useless oil pan on the bus stop bench and tried to catch up with him.

He called back to me, "Get the pan. I smell welding!"

Down an alley, we found an open garage and saw the intermittent flicker of an arc welder. A man in a black hood and a filthy sweatshirt hunched over a table. Sparks flew up from his work.

"Hold," Chuck said, pushing my chest with his forearm. "Not too close. Wait for him to stop. Don't look at the torch."

"I know that," I said, having taken shop in junior high.

The man stopped, took off his helmet and big gloves and used his shirt to wipe his brow, then removed it entirely. As we approached, I couldn't take my eyes off the eagle tattooed across his barrel chest. He dripped with sweat.

"Whataya got dere?" he asked in a thick accent. "Ya. I see," he said as Chuck showed him the hole in the pan. "Not so goot."

"Can it be welded?"

"Of course I fix. Like new. Tomorrow come back."

"Uh, we're on the bus, sir. Can we wait?"

"You brought on bus? Ah! Goot boys," he laughed and nodded. "Ya. You wait."

His wife appeared with tall lemonades. We eagerly accepted. She motioned for us to follow her to a small backyard beside the garage.

"Stay," she said, pointing at a glass garden table.

The welder charged us five dollars. Within an hour, we were returning on the bus with our repaired oil pan across our laps. It still felt warm although he had soaked it in cool water. Scorched but partially visible on the tin he had used to fill the gaping hole, we noticed part of the Budweiser brand name. Chuck traced the weld with his forefinger and commented on the quality of the work. While in town waiting to transfer buses, we found a pawnshop and bought a set of used ratchet wrenches for a couple of bucks. In the end, we repaired Erby for less than ten dollars, counting our bus fare.

"We need a gasket," Chuck explained. "And, there's not going to be anything the right size on the Island. I could write for one, but it would take weeks."

As victory got nearer, his sentences got longer.

"What'll we do for a gasket?"

I had no idea what a gasket did. He explained that it sealed the metal to metal.

"What is it made of?" I asked.

He tried to explain a soft material like a mixture of cork, cloth and rubber. I suggested athletic bandages. Chuck looked at me with a new appreciation.

"That might work."

He carefully placed the oil pan on several thicknesses of rubberized gauze and cut around it with a surgeon's scalpel. Using denture adhesive we borrowed from a friend on the geriatric ward, he stuck the gasket to the bottom rim of the oil pan, put more adhesive on the exposed side, and he replaced it with the original small bolts as I held it in place.

"Need a torque wrench," he whispered as he ratcheted the last in place.

"A dork wrench?" I repeated.

"You know what that is?" he asked.

"Not at all," I admitted.

104

"Doesn't matter. This'll hold till I can get a real gasket. Let's get the oil into this baby."

We made another midnight run to the motor pool to get oil for Erby. We couldn't find any new cans so we hustled back to the hospital and grabbed some empty detergent bottles from the trash. Back at the motor pool, we filled each with drain oil from a barrel. This time, Erby swallowed every quart and digested it all. We siphoned gas from our ambulance and poured it into Erby's tank.

With no one in sight to help us in the middle of the night, Chuck and I exhausted ourselves pushing Erby up an incline out of the parking lot onto the road. Cheshire opened the hood and squirted rubbing alcohol into the carburetor. He said that it would ignite quicker than the gas after sitting dry so long.

"It's an automatic. We can't pop a clutch, so you'll need to shift it into gear when you hit at least twenty miles per hour."

"What? I'm driving?" I asked.

"It's your car. You get the first shot. I'll push to get you going and jump in. When we hit twenty, throw it down into first."

Rolling down the hill, we watched the speedometer. It only reached twenty and I jerked the shift down into the lowest gear. Erby stopped cold without as much as much as a cough.

"Shoot!" Chuck sat and thought. Then he looked over and yelled, "The key, dummy. Turn on the ignition!"

This time, we were at a steeper portion of the hill near the bottom. When he got me going, Chuck couldn't catch me. In the rear-view mirror, I could see him yelling at me to throw it in gear.

I did.

"Ka-blam!!"

Erby sent an explosion backward that could be heard on the top floor of the hospital behind closed windows. It blew

105

back a blue flame that enveloped Chuck. Black smoke billowed out of the exhaust. I stomped down on the accelerator. Erby responded. We outran the smoke. My buddy disappeared from my mirror. I gave it gas at the bottom of the hill and Erby headed around the loop and up the other side. He didn't have a lot of power, but he was running! Completing the full circle, I drove up to Chuck Cheshire still patting at the smoldering in his moustache and the front of his hair.

"Yeehaw!" he shouted as I drove up.

"You're on fire!" I yelled through the open window.

"No big deal," he said, jumping in beside me as we headed off to buy a battery and fill the tank with gas. Behind us, smoke covered the King Kameiameia Highway.

Chuck looked back and said, "Good thing we'll be driving only at night."

Any key could start Erby, and the door locks didn't work, so keeping him to ourselves presented a problem. Chuck disengaged a wire hidden under the starter which rendered the car useless.

"Unless someone knows what they're looking for, this oughta do the trick."

Parking always presented a problem in Waikiki. Our apartment did not come with its own lot, so we would have to find spots on the street. One early morning, we parked in the lot of our local convenience store and walked up the hill a block to get our stuff for the beach. Less than a half hour later, Erby had been towed. The proprietor recognized me and apologized.

"I'm so sorry. When I opened this morning, I thought somebody had parked there all night. I didn't know your car."

We would have to pay the salvage yard for towing and storage, forty-five dollars plus five dollars a day. The longer Erby sat, the more it would cost us. We were already out fifty dollars. Having ten bucks between us until payday, about two weeks away, we were more dejected when we called the yard and the man said he'd sell it for salvage if not picked up within ten days.

"It doesn't start. You can't even hotwire the piece of junk," he explained.

On the tenth day, we returned to the yard shortly after it opened. I did the talking.

"Hello. I'm from the university. We're having a car-smash to raise money. Do you have a car we could have for cheap?"

"Hell, you can have that blue Rambler over there for nothin', if you'll tow it out of here."

"Thank you, sir. That one will do just fine," I said, shaking the man's hand. "May I have something that says it's mine so I can show the dean?"

"I'll give you the state salvage numbered receipt."

"That should do it, sir. Thank you."

After he finished the paperwork, and the junkyard man released the car to us, we all went out to inspect Erby. When the man asked when we'd be back to haul it away, we asked him what time he closed.

"You gotta be back before five."

He walked back to his shack. I held the salvage paperwork in my hand. Chuck replaced the starter wire and we drove Erby out the front gate, right past the man who had a look on his face that I'll never forget.

Sweardagod.

Before I left Hawaii, I had the Volvo removed by a salvage company for ten bucks, and I sold Erby to an army cook for two hundred dollars. He told everybody what a deal he'd made "off some dumb sucker." Right. I'm glad he was happy with his purchase.

Ambulance

Never drive on New Year's Eve. Period. From about ten until three, there isn't one sound driver on the roads. Unless you're intoxicated, why swim against the mainstream? If you're speeding and swerving like the others, you may be relatively safe as you all seem to miss each other. For the rest of us, well, see rule number one.

Vic and I were working ambulance shift at Tripler Army Medical Hospital on the hill overlooking Honolulu. At midnight, the city ignited in a trillion firecrackers lit all at the same instant. Even though safely a few miles away, we couldn't hear ourselves speak for about two minutes. Then, most of the noise subsided rather abruptly, leaving us with ringing in our ears and the rest of a nightshift in front of us.

"No calls tonight," Vic prayed aloud. "A long safe night ahead."

"Heard that," I agreed.

He shouldn't have cursed the gods. At twelve past twelve, we got a call from Admiral Jensen's daughter-in-law. Her voice came out of the speaker on the E.R. desk.

"I'm here alone with Grandpa. Everyone is out. He is having some kind of attack."

"What are his symptoms?" the duty nurse asked.

"He says it's just angina, but he's so pale," she said. "Can you send somebody? I really don't know what to do."

The retired admiral had been in the Emergency Room many times. The duty nurse recognized his name and

109

condition. "He has nitro pills somewhere. Have him put one under his tongue."

"What pills? I don't know where they are."

"He does. He knows what to do."

"Ma'am, I don't think he knows. He heard all the fireworks and thinks they're attacking Pearl Harbor again."

"What is he doing right now," the nurse asked.

"He is talking to his wife, Ma'am."

"Well, ask her to get his nitroglycerin."

The daughter-in-law lowered her voice, "His wife has been dead for thirteen years."

"We'll send an ambulance," the nurse said.

"That's us," Vic moaned. "Bad timing. Bad timing."

"We'll be okay," I said. "I'll drive."

"You bet," Vic agreed. "I'll ride shotgun and watch for low flying drunks."

We took the back road to Fort Shafter and drove through the army base to the retired military neighborhood bordering its south side. Staying off the highway and detouring through the base took extra time, but it reduced the chance of confronting any crazies.

When we arrived, the admiral sat wheezing in a lounge chair. He indeed looked pallid. Vic immediately placed a mask on his face to administer oxygen. I took vitals. The fresh air had the desired affect almost immediately. The admiral breathed deeply, smiled, and gave us a thumbs-up. His daughter relaxed a bit.

"Will you stay?" she asked. "At least until the others come home?"

"We're going to transport him," I said. "His pulse is steady but a little weak. His blood pressure is bouncing around. It's not bad, but if something is trying to happen, we'd rather have him at the hospital."

"I understand. Let me get my purse and leave a note," she said.

Vic and I secured the admiral to our stretcher and slid him into the back of the ambulance. Vic and the daughter sat beside the patient as I drove back to Tripler. I picked up my two-way and called the duty nurse.

"We're bringing him in. Pulse is weak, but normal. Blood pressure is all over the map. Couldn't get a consistent reading. He's responding well to oxygen."

"We'll be standing by," she responded. "I have called the cardiac team, just to be safe."

"They may say we're over-reacting, but I agree," I said. "See you in a few."

The MPs at Fort Shafter monitored all our ambulance calls on their military radios. They paid special attention when we traveled anywhere near or on their base.

"Coming back through Shafter," I said. "You gate jockeys got your ears on?"

"That's a roger, Ambulance One," a young voice responded. "We'll secure this gate and wave you through."

Good. At the north gate where there was a signal, we'd need to turn right onto a city street to take the back road to Tripler. Having a guard in the intersection meant I would have the right-of-way. I tuned on my red lights anyway.

"Okay back there?" I asked Vic.

"He's doing fine. The oxygen is helping."

Coming within sight of the MPs guard gate, I saw that the light facing me was red. I took my foot off the accelerator. No reason to speed. It was a sharp corner. I could wait at the light. In the crossroads, an MP waved his right hand in a circle, directing me to ignore the signal light and come on through. As the distance narrowed, I saw the yellow light come on for cross traffic.

"Whew," I thought. "No hurry at all. New Year's Eve. Take no risks. I'll slow enough to get the green."

The light in my direction turned green at least a hundred feet before I reached the guard station. The attendant stepped out of his door and saluted as I passed.

111

His face and that of his partner in the intersection reflected the flashing lights from our vehicle. They were both smiling. As I slowly turned the corner, a paint truck going over eighty missed the MP by inches and slammed into my left rear quarter.

The ambulance pushed up on its right two wheels and turned what must have looked like a big clumsy pirouette in the street. After a full circle, the tires returned to the road and we came to a hard stop. I never saw the truck. It hit us and careened down a hill to our left, disappearing from view.

The stretcher came out of its restraints which tossed the admiral and Vic on their sides in the back. The oxygen bottle smacked something, broke off the head, and made a terrible screaming sound. I climbed over my seat to help right the stretcher. The admiral began heaving and gasping for breath.

"Get us out of here!" Vic demanded.

I leaped back over the seat and out of my door to survey the damage. The MP from the guard gate arrived at the back fender at the same time as I did. He was no longer smiling.

"It's okay. Pull!" he yelled. Together we ripped the dangling fender away from the wheel well.

"Can I just leave?" I asked.

"Give me your license," he said, holding out his hand. "We'll deal with the police."

"Your partner?" I asked.

"He's chasing the driver down the hill."

"Oh, man. I thought sure he was hit."

"Naw. Missed him by inches. He's pissed, though."

I tossed him my wallet as I got back into the ambulance. When I tried to call the hospital, the radio wasn't working.

"Drive!" the M.P. urged, looking in the back at Vic and his patient.

"Call Tripler," I yelled out my widow. "Radio's out."

112

In my rear-view-mirror, I saw Vic administering CPR to the admiral.

"Hold on," I yelled.

"Let 'er out," Vic yelled. "I'm losing him."

I drove up the hill as fast as the old military ambulance would go, red lights and siren blazing. Approaching the back door to ER, I turned the big land yacht into a four wheel slide and backed up to the loading dock. A team of about twenty people waited. They had the admiral inside on a table within seconds.

"Where's the daughter?" Vic asked as I joined him in the Emergency Room.

"Oh, shoot!" I turned to run back to the ambulance.

When I slid the side door open, the admiral's daughter-in-law fell out on her knees and regurgitated into the driveway.

"Nurse!" I yelled.

A few hours later, a Honolulu Police patrolman stood in front of me.

"Mr. Sherman?" he asked.

"That's me."

"Here's your wallet. Nice thinking, leaving your I.D. I got everything I need here. I just need you to confirm what the MPs told me. Are you okay?"

"We were medics in Vietnam," Vic explained. "Things don't shake us up much anymore."

"Me too," he said. "Not a medic, though. I was with the Shore Patrol."

"Navy?"

"Yep."

"You out now?" Vic asked.

"Naval Reserve," he explained.

He filled me in on the facts about the accident and said that the MP chased the drunk driver on foot for over a mile before he caught the guy and arrested him.

"He'll do some time for this one," the cop explained. "DUI, reckless endangerment, failure to heed, leaving the scene, resisting arrest... and, according to the owner, the truck was also stolen. The driver was forbidden to drive it when not at work."

"Man, talk about getting the book thrown at you," I said.

"He won't be driving anything for a long time. It's a good thing for him that the admiral made it."

"Yeah," Vic agreed. "What would that be? Manslaughter?"

"Somebody dies when you're committing all those other crimes, it can go pretty hard on you. Judges in Hawaii aren't exactly compassionate, y'know."

"I hate driving on New Year's Eve," I said.

"Don't blame you. Me too."

Two years after the accident, forwarded a letter that they received addressed to me at their home. An insurance company in Hawaii wrote me that they had determined I was at fault in a traffic accident with a vehicle owned by their client, a paint company. The only place they could have found my address was the original accident report, which included the official description of the accident, the witness statements, and the numerous citations issued to the driver of the vehicle.

Unbelievable audacity.

My subsequent letter to the police department in Honolulu gave them the date of the accident, which was the only information I had, and a copy of the letter from the insurance agency. I received a quick response from an inspector acknowledging my letter, assuring me that I had nothing to worry about, and thanking me for the full day of laughter I had provided him and his fellow officers.

Cows

For my tenth birthday, my dad took me with him on a two-week trip down the length of California from Sacramento to Los Angeles. We had made the trip before, and I could name every city on old HWY 99: Lodi, Stockton, Manteca, Modesto, Ceres, Keyes, Turlock, Delhi, Livingston, Atwater, Merced, and a hundred others to Fresno and on to Bakersfield, up and over the old Grapevine into L.A. On subsequent trips when my dad would take me out of the boredom of public school to be his travel partner for a week, we counted the disappearing cities and towns and the interruptions of their pesky traffic lights as the modern Interstate replaced the old two-lane highway. From my tenth birthday to our trip south five years later to take my sister to college, that same trip had been reduced from twelve to eight hours. When I-5 looped west around Stockton, that final stretch of super highway eliminated the last stoplights from Tijuana to British Columbia. It cut another half hour off my drive from college in Orange County to home in Sacramento.

My parents retired, down-sized, and moved to their cabin at Lake Tahoe. It added back two hours in driving time. Traveling to see them at Thanksgiving, to make it before dark, I left the city of Orange at seven in the morning. My passenger seat held a six pack of Dr Pepper, three packages of Twinkies, and a box of NoDoz. I knew from experience that I'd get sleepy if I didn't follow a steady regimen of sugar and caffeine.

115

My VW bug topped out at exactly seventy-nine miles per hour on flat land. I pressed the accelerator to the floor and kept it there for seven hours. As I left the hills coming out of the L.A. basin and hit the long straight road running north through the San Joaquin Valley, the FM radio stations faded out and I talked to myself out loud, repeating the entire history of my life from my very first recollections. With nobody listening, I embellished and elaborated, making mountains of mole hills, giving details that would certainly bore anyone but me. I raised and lowered my voice and used numerous dialects and accents in acting out all of the characters in my life saga. By Stockton, I ran out of story, snacks, soda pop, and gas. Buzzing from the stimulants, I filled the VW, gulped down another couple of NoDoz using the warm residue in a couple of spent Dr Peppers, and pressed pedal to metal to make the final three hours to Tahoe.

In Auburn, the first snowfall of the season began as a gentle caress. In my cozy bug, I hadn't even noticed the temperature dropping twenty degrees in as many miles. By Colfax, thick soft flakes the size of coasters hit my windshield and tested my wipers. The road turned white, and I concentrated on staying within the two lines left by traffic before me. Soon, the tracks got lighter. By Bastrop, still at least thirty miles from the summit, the pavement disappeared. One-by-one, cars and trucks pulled off the road to wrestle with their dreaded chains.

"Aw, come one, you chickens!" I yelled from my cocoon. "It ain't that bad yet."

I hate putting on chains. It kills my fingers. If you don't catch the latch behind the wheel on the first try, your fingers freeze. To avoid this, I would rather jack up the car, take the wheels off to attach the chains securely. But, the summit wasn't *that* far away. I'd driven in worse.

"Don't stop!" I pleaded.

116

I needed all their tires forging ahead of me, not on the side of the road.

"The Highway Patrol will tell us when to pull over," I yelled, passing by the faint hearted.

With the windshield wipers on high, I opened my window a crack for fresh air, and fell in behind an eighteen-wheeler returning to the highway after having installed his chains. Momentarily, at least, the ruts behind the truck remained a shade of grey. The trucker kept his speed steady at exactly twenty for at least an hour. Then, inexplicably, he drove over to the side of the road and slowed to a stop. I followed him and waited. After a few minutes, his headlights and taillights went dark but the running lights remained lit. I put on my coat and cap. Outside, I saw the driver climb down out of the cab.

Moving toward me, a woman in jeans and a plaid jacket shouted, "Closin' 'er down!" He was a she.

I looked forward and back. There were no other vehicles going either way. She had picked a place where the shoulder widened and her truck sat well off the highway.

"You wanna come on up?" she asked. "I'm keepin' 'er runnin' fer heat."

"I declined. "Thanks a lot. I'll wait for another truck to follow."

She stood there looking at me, shook her head, and returned to the front where she climbed up into the warm cab giving me a hearty wave. She leaned over and let go with a stream of tobacco juice before she closed the door. I shuddered.

I eased the accelerator and released the clutch at the same time, pulled the steering wheel left, slipped out of the ruts left by the truck, and found myself on pure white highway. The painted lines had disappeared. My usual navigation senses didn't work. This being the first snowfall, there were no ridges on the sides of the road left by snow removal. The highway in front of me looked like an open lake of powder. Keeping it under about fifteen avoided fishtailing. Fortunately, the snowfall stopped and the sky in front of me looked lighter. I could make out the markers on the right shoulder. It would soon be getting dark. The summit had to be near.

"Omagod! A cow!"

Right in the center of the road in front of me stood a full grown cow. It swiveled its big head to look at me as the VW slid to a stop.

"Mooo," it said, almost indignantly.

"God Almighty, there is a cow and it is mooing in the middle of the road!"

Nobody could hear me shouting. The cow looked unimpressed. She had problems of her own. She didn't seem to know whether to go forward or back. She kept looking around as if asking for directions. I probably looked like another cow, a fat green one, and she moved toward me. I politely beeped my horn.

That might not have been the best idea. The cow bolted and skidded on the icy pavement sending her legs flailing in all directions to regain balance. Her momentum brought her directly toward my little beetle. Fortunately, before she made contact, her body regained its limited bovine composure, and she walked deliberately past my driver's side window as if insulted. I put the car in gear and slid around her before heading straight again.

Four more cows. Right in my path. Live cows!

They moved from left to right about ten feet in front of me. Now I realized how much heavier than my VW Bug they each were. Out of nowhere, from the right, a fifth cow raised up on her back legs, lunged forward, and head-butted the lead cow. I'd never seen anything like it. To me, cows were normally part of the picturesque serene landscape, either walking slowly or immobile. Like two mountain goat rams, except without the horns, they smashed heads. From inside my airtight car, I heard skulls cracking. This sent a fright right through me. I eased on the accelerator to pass behind these beasts who were obviously not acting like themselves.

Visibility increased, and I could see landscape separating my east-bound lanes from those coming down out of the Sierras. A couple dozen or more cattle wandered around the wide highway divider. Cordovan cows were everywhere. Some stood motionless. Others roamed in different directions. I forgot about the icy road and steered wildly around several more cows that had made it up to my side of the divided highway. Slipping and sliding, I avoided each animal. I felt like a running back with the football under my arm and six linemen between me and the goal line.

"Oh give me a home," I sang out loud, "where the buffalo don't roam."

On the other side of the freeway, traffic had stopped behind a blazing cattle truck. Flames engulfed the length of the carrier. The unhitched cab had been moved safely away from the trailer. Several men stood on the side of the road helpless to do anything about the uncontrolled fire. The stray cows, now dotting the landscape in every direction, had been frightened by the fire, hence the atypical head-butting. I didn't need to cause further panic by approaching them with what probably resembled a green beast to them. I slowed to a crawl.

Filling my rearview mirror, a Fiat sports car appeared. For over an hour, I had been alone in the eastbound lanes. In the few moments it took to dodge the cows, a man had caught up with me and followed off my rear bumper. I could plainly see his face in my mirror. His eyes were white against his dark skin. A turban hid his hair. He leaned forward to where his face appeared a couple of inches from his windshield. I made eye contact, and he nodded his head eagerly. He had no intention of letting me get more than ten feet ahead of him.

Looking ahead, I saw a frightful sight. Coming downhill from the opposite direction, flying across the median, a large sedan loaded with passengers headed sideways directly at me in a four-wheel-slide. The driver frantically spun the steering wheel right and left, but nothing stopped his path toward my tiny bug. Time stood still. Snow flew from his wheel wells as the land-yacht blew through the new fallen powder. I could feel the crash before it happened, and instinctively jammed into first gear and popped the clutch, pulling my steering wheel to the right. My little car literally jumped out of the way. I watched the driver's face as it flew past less than a yard from mine. Then I shut my eyes, hunched my shoulders, and ducked my head anticipating the terrible collision about to happen behind me.

Nothing. No sound. It missed both of us. I lifted my head to look in the mirror and saw the Fiat driver, his face showing panic. His knuckles were white on the steering wheel. He blinked a dozen times and nodded again.

"Let's go," he seemed to be saying.

Driving steadily toward the summit, the small sports car remained a few feet behind me. The snow stopped, but the road still showed no relief from a blanket of white. I fishtailed a few times, but regained control and looked back to see if my follower remained there. Yep, right behind me, not gaining or losing as much as a yard.

We made the high point and cautiously negotiated the curves and slopes for another hour down the other side until we arrived in Truckee. Snow plows were just entering the freeway headed west, back to where we had been. I exited at the turn-off to Tahoe and stopped at a gas station. As I stepped out, the other driver immediately confronted me, looking up past outstretched praying hands.

"Afendi!" he greeted me. "Fine drivah! Praise and thanks!"

"Uh?"

"All praise to Allah!"

"OK. Yes."

"Allah be praised. Excellent drivah!"

He backed all the way to his vehicle, bowing as he went. Following a wave of his clasped hands and another prayer that had something to do with my continued safety, he shot back up the onramp toward Reno.

My parents' cabin waited still a half-hour away, and the snowing had resumed. As the adrenaline subsided, my body reminded me painfully of many hours of caffeine and sugar. My eyes burned and my stomach reacted to every turn in the road. My heartbeat about doubled.

The last street to my parents' cabin is straight up, then down, then up again and around a sharp turn. The snowplow hadn't been there yet.

"No way I'm putting on chains for the last block!" I said aloud, leaning as close as I could to the front window. "Give 'er the gas!"

I took the first corner as fast as I dared, accelerated down the hill, barely had enough momentum to make it up the next hill, and slid sideways safely into their driveway. I left everything in the car and ran into the house, speaking excitedly.

"I'm here! I'm safe! It's OK. Not to worry. Long drive. Stopped once for gas. Dr Pepper kept me going. A little dicey there for a bit. Snow from the foothills. Cows in the road. Live cows! Big truck fire. Two butted heads. Almost smacked by a maniac coming downhill too fast in a land yacht! Slid right by me. Missed by inches. Sweardagod! Lucky to be here. Little sports car guy behind me, eyes popping out of his head, bowed and praised Allah. No problem. I'm great now. Just need to rest and get some water. How you doing?"

Mom had a pile of yarn in her lap, and dad sat reading. The fire crackled behind the Boston Pops playing low from speakers in all four corners of the room.

"Are you hungry, dear?" she asked.

"Hello, son," my dad said. "Glad you're home."

"Wash your hands," my mother said. "I'll fix you something."

Smythe

Most people think of Texas as a flat desert. This is true for about eighty percent of the land mass, the area called West Texas. Except for a few oasis towns, there's a lot of dirt out there without much relief. However, Central Texas around Austin and San Antonio is a land of rolling hills and scrub oak trees, spotted with lakes and rivers. East Texas is another surprise. Between Dallas and Houston, along the border with Louisiana, hides a beautiful little city under tall pines called Nacogdoches. It is the home of Stephen F. Austin State University. After attending a weekend retreat there, I decided to take the long way home. My map showed a wiggly blue line meandering west to my home in Georgetown. Having driven through West Texas several times, I took this opportunity to see a greener side of the state through backwoods giving way to open rolling hills with many farms and ranches. I'm glad I took the extra time to see the "other" Texas, and I got to meet all of the residents of one small town.

Cruising along virtually alone on the two-lane highway, I almost missed the sign that read "Smythe, Population 4."

Sweardagod. Four. It had to have cost more to make the sign and install it than the taxes a town of four might produce in a year. Taking my foot off the accelerator didn't slow my car quickly enough. If I didn't apply the brakes hard, I'd sail right by the only two structures.

On my right appeared a small market with two gas pumps. About a hundred feet behind the building stood a forty-foot mobile home. Two dirt paths led from doors at each end of the trailer around to each side of the market. As I stopped in front, I saw that the gas pumps had not been in working order for many years. They stood stolidly, showing the faded paint of harsh winters. Their hoses and nozzles were missing. Empty holes in the ground showed where water and air once were provided. A faint hand-scrawled sign on the glass of one of the pumps stated tersely, "NO GAS PERIOD!"

There were no posters in the window, no newspaper racks, and none of the usual neon or fluorescents of a convenience store. In fact, there were no signs at all. Obscured by years of neglect, the front windows were brownish yellow with tobacco residue from the interior.

The screen door protested loudly as I pushed it open. Two older women in flower print dresses sat on stools at opposite ends of a long counter. They had fifteen feet of bare space between them. On the left corner of the counter, beside a cash register, sat an inverted hubcap with at least a hundred cigarette filters sticking up out of the sand. On the right end of the same counter, I saw a mirror image, an identical register, with another hubcap and scores of filters sticking out of the sand. The only difference appeared to be the print on the dresses and the color of the cigarette filters.

Two ladies, two cash registers, two ashtrays, and nothing else on the long counter. Behind them on the wall, a cigarette display had only two brands for sale. A sign taped to the middle of the case repeated the message from outside. "No gas. Not now. Not tomorrow."

I walked down the aisles of their store. The shelves were bare. The refrigeration cases were dark. I found an open carton of Hostess Twinkies and took one package. There were two bags of pretzels and a cylinder of oatmeal, some work gloves, and a plastic model airplane in a sealed box. That was it.

Taking my Twinkies to the counter, I handed a dollar bill to the woman on the right side. She rang up my purchase and shoved my change across the counter without leaving her stool or saying a word.

"Well, this must be half the population of the town of Smythe," I said with my best Texas neighborly smile.

A long pause ensued. I stood holding my snack feeling like a Twinkie myself. Finally, the woman on the left released me from the tension.

"This is the *whole* town," she twanged.

"Really?" I asked. "The sign said population four."

"Men done run off," the lady in front of me explained.

Sweardagod. You can visit yourself, and I bet they're still there.

They both frowned harshly. I couldn't imagine doubling my time in Smythe by remaining another two minutes.

One bite of the Twinkies told me I should have read the expiration date.

Corpse

Why is a dead body creepy? People are universally more frightened of a lifeless body than a charging rhino. It's make no logical sense, but scary is scary, and we don't know why.

Working the night shift at Tripler Hospital in Hawaii, I went down to the cafeteria for my regular wee hours breakfast and found the two guys from the morgue sitting in a trance, gulping coffee, trying to reclaim their breath.

"What's up in graveyard on graveyard?" I asked, smiling at my wee hour wit.

Their response came more visually than vocally as their rolling eyes underscored unintelligible grunts and shaking heads. It took me awhile to get the story out of them.

A body came down from ICU, and they had rolled it over to one of the morgue drawers. These night guys didn't do any embalming, they merely received, inventoried, and stored bodies.

The drawer wouldn't open. A cadaver jammed it from the inside. They explained to me that muscles can contract after life has expired. As they opened the drawers on the right and left, they could see that a body had stiffened into a partial sitting position on the slab directly below. Its head and knees blocked the sliding mechanism of the drawer above.

They tried to push down on the chest, but the muscles wouldn't relax. They pulled out the drawers on each side of the body, and both of them crawled onto the adjacent slabs, one feet first, the other head first. They each rolled into position adjacent to the body.

"One, two... push!"

Their story stopped for a moment of reflection. They looked at each other, mimicking their horror, and shook their whole bodies.

"Aagh!"

"As we both pushed down, the muscles all relaxed, and air pushed up out of the lungs through the larynx," one of them explained.

"Oohhhhhh!" they both exclaimed, repeating the guttural sound the corpse had made.

"Next thing I remember was the sound of my shoes slapping against the hall floor!" one said.

"And the sound of heavy panting. My panting. His panting," the other added.

They ran all the way to the cafeteria and were sitting down with their coffee before their senses kicked in, and they saw me walking up to their table.

"What about the body?" I asked.

"He's still lying in there with the drawers open."

"Yeah. He ain't goin' anywhere."

As other late workers came to breakfast, I asked the guys to retell their story. We all talked about our natural reactions to dead bodies. Everyone agreed that it's interesting how people fear death, as if it were some unknown phenomenon rather than a normal fact of life. Nobody gets out of here alive. Why all the fuss?

A few years earlier, my brother-in-law was involved in a corpse caper. I shared the story with my morgue friends that morning.

Stuart's friend, Steve, called him late on a Friday evening.

"Whatcha doing tonight?"

"Nothing. You got a better idea?"

"Need some help with a stiff."

Steve worked for a funeral home. When a person was near the end, the family often made arrangements with the mortuary to retrieve the body as soon after death as possible.

"My hearse broke down," Steve explained to Stuart. "I'm at a phone booth about ten miles out of Orange. The head gasket blew. I have no power at all."

"Where were you going?"

"Picking up a body in Riverside. The coroner is waiting at the house. He gave me the address but no phone number. I need to get there."

"Riverside? Why don't they call somebody closer?"

"We're doing the funeral here. Are you going to drive me or not?"

"In my Ford?" Stuart asked.

"The deceased won't mind," Steve said. "I'm stuck. If you can't help, I need to call somebody else right away."

"I'm there, man. Where are you, exactly?"

Stuart drove his '56 Ford two-door coupe a few miles out of town and found his buddy leaning against a smoldering black hearse.

"Thanks, partner. I'm buying breakfast."

In the early Sixties, traffic on the old two-lane Highway 55 to Riverside didn't amount to much in the late hours. Known for his small-town dirt-track mentality and his hot car, Stuart raced through the evening. He wasted no time getting to Riverside.

"They'll wait," his shaky passenger cried. "The guy can't get any deader, but we can!"

"This is good for the engine," Stu assured him. "Burns the carbon off the valves."

Steve leaned over to look at the speedometer.

"Can you keep it under a hundred, please?" he begged. "I don't want us to end up on one of my slabs tonight."

"Trust me," Stuart smiled. "I'm not even top-end yet."

They got to Riverside about when expected. The county coroner thought the Ford a bit unorthodox, but had no other option.

"The family left awhile ago," he said. "Who's to notice in the middle of the night?"

They thanked him for his help lifting the heavy body into the car. Stuart cranked up the Ford and sped toward home. About fifteen miles out of Riverside, they passed a hitchhiker. The two buddies looked at each other as Stu took his foot off the accelerator.

"No," Steve pleaded.

"Right," Stu agreed.

He hit the gas again.

There is a thin line between depraved humor and just plain wickedness. Stuart will insist that he felt sorry for the guy, that he remembered hitching many times late at night when no one would stop. He'll swear that his right foot came off the accelerator and hit the brakes from sheer compassion and generosity for a fellow human being in need. We know better. His motivation came from nowhere near sympathy. Stuart had a dead guy in the back seat.

He spun a U-turn, sending dust flying off both sides of the road. He slowly passed the hitchhiker, checking him out. A hundred yards in the opposite direction, Stu flipped another u-turn.

"Prop the guy up," Stuart told Steve.

"Are you kidding?"

"Come on. We're gonna need some room back there."

Steve crawled back over his seat, picked up the guy by his coat and propped him against the side window behind the driver's seat. The Ford slowed to a stop right by the outstretched thumb.

"Where ya headed?"

"Santa Ana."

Steve grimaced at the smell of alcohol fuming from the man's mouth.

"Hop in!" Stuart smiled. "We can take you as far as Orange."

"Right on!" The man opened the door and pushed the passenger seat forward to crawl into the back. "Orange is close enough. How y'all doin'?"

"Bitchin'," Stuart beamed, hitting the gas and leaving a thousand pebbles flying behind.

Steve and the corpse didn't say anything.

Stuart reached up to adjust his rear-view mirror so he could keep an eye on the back. The hitchhiker pulled out a small brown paper sack and twisted off the lid of a half-pint bottle. He gulped hard with a quick jerk of his neck and replaced the cap clumsily.

"Hey, buddy," the guy in the back said to his partner, "Wanna hit?"

He offered the bottle across the seat receiving, of course, no reply.

"I say, you wanna *drink*?" he repeated to the corpse.

Agitated at being ignored, he slid a bit closer. Steve looked at Stuart who had his rapt attention on the drama unfolding in the mirror.

"Stu?" Steve pleaded. "Watch the road."

Stuart brought his forefinger to his lips.

"Hey buddy! I asked you if you wanted a *drink?*"."

The drunk gave the corpse a gentle shove in the arm. "You too good to drink with an old road man like me?"

The body fell toward him landing face down in the man's lap. In a panic, he pushed the corpse back to its original position and slid as far as he could to the right side.

"Hey! What's wrong with your buddy here?" he hollered. "He ain't right."

"Don't mess with him," Stuart said. "He's been dead since early this evening."

"STOP THE CAR! LET ME OUT!" The hitchhiker threw the seat forward, slamming Steve into the dashboard.

Stuart hit the brakes hard and pulled over to the shoulder. Before they fully stopped, the passenger grabbed the handle, opened the door, and lunged out of the car. He landed with a roll on the side of the road, and scrambled to his feet. He ran off like a madman.

Stuart and Steve shrieked with laughter all the way back to Orange. When they topped the short hill bordering suburbia, they saw a highway filled with flashing red lights.

"Yikes!" Stuart yelled. "What the heck is that?"

"Must be a terrible crash," Steve said.

"I've never seen so many cops."

They slowed to a crawl approaching a roadblock.

"PULL OVER!" came over a loudspeaker.

Stuart stopped in front of several patrol cars. Uniformed police leaned over the hoods of their cars, pistols drawn.

"Somebody is expecting us," Stuart said.

"It's OK," Steve replied. "I know most of these guys."

"PUT YOUR HANDS OUTSIDE YOUR WINDOWS."

"Well, maybe not all of them," Steve said, pushing his hands out the driver's window.

"FREEZE RIGHT THERE."

"What about the guy in the back?" Stuart asked Steve. "If he doesn't show his hands, they might shoot him."

"Please don't joke," Steve asked.

Flashlights hit both of their faces.

"Oh, it's Steve!" one of the cops said. *"STAND DOWN!"* he hollered to the others.

Steve got out to talk to the officer. Many of the cops knew him as the hearse driver in funerals they escorted. As soon as they saw his face, the body in the backseat at least appeared legal, if not a bit unusual.

"What are you doing in this coupe?"

"Hearse broke down. I had to call my buddy Stu."

"Oh, I should have known. I saw your rig on the side of the road earlier. I didn't put it together."

The red lights went off. Cops holstered their weapons and moved their squad cars to the side of the road. A few of them joined Stuart and Steve who explained the events of their evening. Laughter rang out as they got to the part about the hitchhiker offering booze to the corpse.

"He called the sheriff," an officer explained.

Flying down the hill behind them, a single highway patrol car interrupted their story with a siren piercing the quiet night air. It came to a screeching halt about fifty feet from the assembly. Two uniformed men leaped out and one of them opened a back door.

The hitchhiker stumbled out screaming, wagging his finger wildly. "That's the car! Those are the murderers!" he shouted. "Arrest them! Why are you all standing around?"

The cops in the street joined Steve and Stu in laughter, and the hitchhiker had to be subdued, but the old guy in the Ford who was to blame for the whole fiasco just sat in the back saying nothing.

Chutzpah

Growing up across the street from the Weinbergs, I occasionally got Yiddish lessons. An expression they used to describe me was "chutzpah" meaning I had over-stepped the boundaries of accepted behavior with seemingly no fear or shame. It sounded like disapproval, but their faces gave away their grudging admiration for my juvenile audacities.

As a nine-year-old, it only took me an hour of sitting at a lemonade stand in front of my house, bored with the lack of passers-by, to realize that I would do better at a busy shopping center. I stacked an ice cooler, three gallons of lemonade, a folding chair and a table on my wagon.

Looking out her kitchen window, Lil Weinberg called my mother to ask if she knew what I was doing. When Mom caught up with me half way down the block, she said, "Well, Lil is right. You certainly have some chutzpah."

It took me more time to get there and set up my stand than it took to sell all the cold fresh lemonade. Call it what you want, I'm not one for passive acceptance. There's nothing quite like taking a risk and coming out ahead.

Magazines

Big Joe Larson stretched his legs across his wood desk showing the bottoms of bigger shoes than I'd ever seen.
"How old are you?"
"Sixteen last month," I said, lying through my teeth.
"Sixteen?"
"Yes, sir"
"Got your driver's license?"
"Just a temporary. I got a hundred on both the written and the driving. I don't have the permanent license yet."
"Show me the real one when you get it."
The thick smoke that filled the office pricked my eyes. I hoped this interview would be brief.
"Be here tomorrow before four. We leave at four every day. You get here at one minute late, you don't work. Understand? Four o'clock! We go by that clock over there."
He pointed at a huge black-rimmed clock on the wall.
"Repeat that back."
"Four o'clock. Got it, sir. Thank you, Mister, uh?"
"Larson, you twit. Big Joe Larson."
"Thank you, Mr. Larson. Four tomorrow, I'll be here."
"A buck and a half an hour plus bonuses. You get paid Friday ever other week. You miss work without telling me, and you don't come back. Get it?"
"Got it!"
He tried to break his desperation with yet another underage innocent by pretending to smile, but it came out as a nasty smirk. His right bicuspid flashed. I'd never seen a

137

real gold tooth before. I couldn't turn my eyes away. Noticing my gawking, he closed his mouth.

"Everyone calls me Big Joe," he said, relighting his pipe.

"See you tomorrow, Mr. Larson,"

"Big Joe!" he repeated with emphasis. "Twit!"

No way would I ever dare call him Big Joe to his face. He intimidated me. I didn't even ask about the work.

A lone guy waiting in the outer office asked me if I knew anything about selling magazines. Ah, that's it. He asked me where I went to high school. I told my third lie in the less than three minutes.

"McClatchy High."

I had just passed my fourteenth birthday. I went to Joaquin Miller Junior High. I wouldn't be in high school for two years.

"We killed you guys in football."

"Right. We're terrible."

"Whadaya drive?" he asked.

"A bike," I said, frowning. "That's why I'm working. I'm saving up."

"Me too. I took the bus."

Over a year away from getting my first learner's permit, I had, in fact, already been driving whenever the opportunity arose. My greatest passion lay behind the wheel. I would agree to any excuse to throw a shift and hit the gas. My sister's boyfriends, three years older, hollered with glee as I hurled their old beaters around the streets of Sacramento. The gearboxes were so slushy, I could hardly miss. The worn shock absorbers had my occupants rolling around in uncontrolled laughter. Fuzzy dice. Suicide knobs. AM radio blaring Buddy Holly and Elvis Presley.

"Benny, you're gonna kill us all!"

With total command at all times, I knew how to hit the imaginary seam just inside the safety zone.

"Leave him be! He's a better driver than any of us."

138

I lived to drive. Meanwhile, it seemed like fifty years till my sixteenth birthday.

The next day, hiding my bike behind the building, I walked into the Home Reader Service at exactly ten to four.

Big Joe loaded eight of us into his Country Squire Ford station wagon and drove us out of central Sacramento, away from our own neighborhoods, to suburbia – Rancho Cordova, Arden, Carmichael, North Sacramento, Fair Oaks – and unloaded us two to a street. We canvassed both sides in tandem, hitting every house.

We carried "surveys" with titles of magazines and little boxes next to each. Our memorized spiel went like this: *"Hello, ma'am. My name is Ben. I live here in the neighborhood. I'm earning money to go to summer camp in the mountains. I've never seen the mountains before, so I wonder if you could help me."*

Sweardagod.

If the lady of the house didn't respond affirmatively immediately, we were told to thank her, smile big, and get to the next door.

"I have a survey here made up by publishers, and all they want to know is what kind of magazines you like. This helps them decide where to advertise."

Hand her the card.

Funny how easy this sounds, but this is the point where a housewife has to open the door. It's a telling moment. I learned to slip the card between the door and the sill so they'd have no concern about safety. We could do all our business with the screen door securely latched.

"If you'd check off your four favorites, that's all they want. Just four you read once in awhile."

She would usually get this far with me. If she needed help, I could throw in *"Like when you were at the beauty parlor today, what magazine did you pick up to read?"*

OK, that wasn't part of the authorized spiel. I did that one on my own. Inevitably, her fingers would fly up and run through her tresses as she blushed. I'd smile back and feign admiring a head of hair which, by the way, looked like it hadn't seen a salon in a decade. A fourteen-year-old can be darn charming when not grossing out girls by eating bugs.

I hit the sales water like a duck.

"And, so they don't think I just filled these out myself, please print your name and address on the card to verify that we talked. Thank you."

This is where Big Joe insisted we throw in another big smile. "Smiling is ninety percent of this work," he reminded us every day.

"If you don't mind adding your phone number, sometimes my boss calls people to be sure I was polite."

"Well you certainly are, honey."

By now, they wanted me off their porch before dinner burned and Daddy came home. They had their compliment for the month.

"And could you sign it please?"

Some people check everything before they sign. It's a very good idea. The housewives in the neighborhoods where Larson drove his masqueraders didn't read the fine print right above their signature. It very plainly said:

"For the purpose of receiving the periodicals checked above for a continuous period of thirty-six months, I the undersigned agree to provide the sum balance due in full for each subscription in one pre-payment as attested by my signature fixed hereto."

If the card came back through the crack with a signature, I thanked the lady profusely and backed away, bowing at the waist. I asked her what smelled so good coming from the kitchen, and hollered "That's my favorite!" over my shoulder and that I'd ask my mom to cook it for me when I got home. I shot off to the next house. Seldom did a door take more than three minutes. If she resisted in the slightest, I made any excuse to exit.

"Just leave," Big Joe warned as he drove us to the neighborhoods. "You got other houses waiting. She dithers at all, don't waste your time, and *my* time."

"Say I gotta catch up with the others," one of the fellas offered.

"And just *leave*," we all piped in.

"Excellent!" sang our driver.

"Say I gotta pee!" one of the guys laughed.

"No!" Big Joe warned, "That'll get you invited in and time's wasting. Plus, what if the old man comes home? What're you gonna do when he walks in on you in his bathroom with your Wet Willy in your hand?"

We all laughed like crazy.

Joe Larson knew how to get us up for the prey. He had us believing in ourselves. We were a team of independent and confident kids. As teenagers, our lives were fraught with submission and compliance at school and at home. Big Joe proffered mirth, irreverence, and a bit of disdain for the adult population. He liberated us from those who dominated us. He replaced the teacher we wish we had in school and offered a welcome relief to our strict parents. Afternoons with this "cool" older guy gave us a daily dose of uncensored enjoyment.

"Never been hungry a day in my life, boys."

"You ever had girls working for you?"

"Never! Girls talk too much," he snapped. "They do one house an hour."

We loved that. We imitated our fairer sex schoolmates chatting up ladies on porches instead of getting the card signed and running off to the next victim.

"I just love your nails."

"How do you tease your hair so high?"

"Do you need a babysitter?"

"I'm going to be a mother and have fifteen children,'' Big Joe added. "And name them all after flowers."

We fell all over the seats in thigh-slapping hilarity.

"Somebody new's waiting for ya' right next door," Big Joe sang. "Never let the grass grow under your shoes."

Joe set a daily goal of ten cards apiece. In only my third week, my best day reaped twenty-seven signed surveys. Big Joe said I had broken a record and he gave me a five-dollar cash bonus right there in the car in front of everybody. He said my name would be in the national registry until somebody else beat my best. Minimum wage in 1960 had reached an all-time high of $1.15 per hour. Five bucks looked like a pot of gold.

"You're gonna be famous," he grinned.

Joe stacked cards on the dashboard. As he drove us back to Oak Park, he shuffled through the daily rewards and looked at the road infrequently. When we hit seventy surveys in a single afternoon, he stopped at an A&W and bought us all tall root beers.

"Set 'em up for my boys!" he ordered the proprietor.

My first paycheck was for fifty-one dollars and fifty cents exactly. Other than being the most money I had ever received in one lump, why would I remember that amount? Because I put fifty dollars in my savings account, bought a fifty-cent cigar, and lit it with a dollar bill. I felt like the king of the world. The older guys laughed as my face turned green. All the way home, my bike's front wheel wobbled.

After I'd been there six months, we hit a bump in the road and we didn't get to say goodbye to Big Joe. Half way through our daily soliciting in Roseville, a slow rolling squad car stopped my block partner and me. A uniformed officer asked what we were doing.

"Working for the Home Reader Service," we said.

"Come with me boys," he said.

We were soon in a small room with our six buddies in the Roseville Police Station looking like deflated balloons.

"Each of you needs to call your parents to come get you," an officer instructed.

I called my dad at work and told him what happened. He said he'd be there as soon as he could. My father carried a badge. He worked for the California Youth Authority. He knew just about every cop, parole or probation officer, judge, prosecutor and public defender in the county. I shuddered at the ghastly look on my dad's face as he found me in the Roseville station.

"Were you booked?" he asked.

"They took us right off the street. I don't know where Mr. Larson is."

"Did they take your fingerprints?"

"No. We've all been sitting right here. They just asked for our names and where we work."

He smiled, "Good."

The police had no interest in us. The name and address of our employer satisfied their inquiry. They didn't even ask us what we were soliciting. I guess they knew. They released each of us to our parents.

My dad talked to the officer in charge for a few minutes and told me on the way home that Mr. Larson had not obtained the proper permit to work in Roseville, a minor offense fixed by filling out a form.

Curiously though, Big Joe vanished when the police cruised the neighborhood. He didn't come down to the station, and the police couldn't reach him at his Oak Park office. Dad said he'd keep an eye on the Home Reader Service, but he didn't suggest that I end my employment. He liked me working after school.

The following day, I showed up alone at the second floor offices. I guessed that the other parents kept their sons home. Picking up your kid at a police station would be a strain on anybody.

"Hiya, kid," popped a rotund man sitting in Joe Larson's office. "You seen Big Joe?"

"No, sir," I said. "He's not here?"

"Station wagon's here, but no Joe. Guess we got the day off."

He lingered awhile.

"What do you do?" I asked.

"I'm a closer, kid," he offered. "I'm the guy who makes the sales."

"How come I never saw you before?"

He explained that Big Joe wanted the closers out of the office before the kids arrived each day. I didn't have to probe much. This guy seemed ready and willing to talk.

"We hit the neighborhoods a week after you boys. We take a contract out to the house for people to sign. It's a National Distributing House contract. Home Reader Service don't even exist, really. Not officially."

"Home Reader Service pays me every two weeks," I argued.

"You ever look at your check?" he asked.

"What do you mean?"

"Big Joe's real careful not to leave any tracks. That's a bank check, not payroll. Did you see any payroll numbers on it? You see any deductions?"

"Deductions?"

"Anybody can have a bank account named anything they want."

"What are deductions?"

"You're priceless, kid. Now I know why Big Joe hires youngsters."

Lou Sanders introduced himself to me, and I relaxed a little. I told him my name too, and he recognized it.

"You're a hellavu card collector!" he said.

Sanders asked me to tell him my technique.

"I just do like Mr. Larson says," I explained. "It wasn't too hard to memorize the spiel."

Lou liked bridging the gap that Joe had created between us. He explained that he and another guy named Battle were the real salesmen. We kids got housewives to sign up for

144

magazines without knowing. The two closers used guilt or fear to get them to sign a valid contract.

"It goes like this," he said. "I show 'em the card. Clear and simple, they signed up for four magazine subscriptions. They always holler that the kid said it's only a survey. He didn't say nuttin 'bout buying nuttin."

Sanders became more animated.

"I love this next part. I show 'em their own signature. POW! They get all slobbery. Some of 'em even whimper a little, and I don't care one bit. It's bidness, y'see. It's a tough world for *all* of us."

This was news to me and it showed.

"Then, I get all serious with 'em. Like this ..."

He pinched his face.

"I drop my hammer on 'em. Battle's got his own way, but I like mine better. I say, 'Why that little brat. He didn't tell you straight out he's sellin' magazines to go to camp? I'll whip his butt when I see him'."

He laughed out loud at this.

"And, they always say, 'No, wait. He *did* say something about camp'."

"And, I say, 'Oh, that's better. Well, he's selling magazines to go up to the mountains. Most of these kids ain't never *seen* the mountains'. That gets most of 'em. That mountain thing works real good. Big Joe come up with it."

My jaw dropped open.

"So I apologize for you kids bein' shy about sellin' stuff. And, they apologize for almost gettin' you in trouble."

Lou laughed at himself again, a forced hoarse laugh.

"And we just keep on makin' each other feel a lot better while they sign the forms and I land us another sucker!"

He guffawed until he coughed up something into a severely soiled handkerchief.

"Ugh," he said, looking in the hanky.

Realizing he'd told me more than I needed to know, Sanders made a hasty exit saying he'd try again tomorrow.

"When does Big Joe usually get here?" I asked, wondering if I'd ever see my paycheck.

"Twelve thirty every day, like clockwork," Lou said at the door. "We do all our calling in the afternoons when babies are napping and before the kids come home from school. I been waitin' here since noon today. I need to pick up more survey cards. But, it's almost four thirty now, and looks like Big Joe ain't gonna show."

"How many people sign contracts?" I asked.

"If we get twenty percent, Joe's happy. I've been doin' a little better than that lately."

We left together.

On my bike, it took twenty minutes to get back and forth to Oak Park from school. The next day, I took off during my lunch hour and got to the Home Reader Service at twelve-twenty. Nothing looked different from when I had left the previous afternoon. I noticed Joe's station wagon still sitting in the parking lot behind the row of businesses. No Joe. No Lou Sanders. At twenty to one, I could wait no longer. I pedaled like mad back to school.

At four o'clock that afternoon, I went back and sat alone in the office again. I peeked in desk drawers for any evidence that would suggest the Home Reader Service still existed. I found a checkbook with a neatly printed register showing a balance of over three thousand dollars. The last entry in the register didn't match the next check available, however, and the last check wasn't recorded.

I found a hand-written list with phone numbers and addresses. A few dozen names had lines drawn through them, and I recognized the names of my partners in the street. On the reverse side were numbers for Lou Sanders and Frank Battle. Dozens of other names and numbers on the back were crossed out. Letters in a neat stack filled a side drawer, each addressed to the Home Reader Service. A few were from the Bank of America, Oak Park Branch, but most were from the National Distribution Service of

Canton, Ohio. They listed names of magazines opposite amounts in the right column. At the bottom of each letter, a line said: "Enclosed remittance for," and included a dollar amount. Blank survey cards sat in a neat stack in the second drawer. The third drawer had subscription forms. I assumed they were the ones the closers used. In the shallow middle drawer, I found only pencils and a pad. But, as I slid it shut, I heard something jangle in the back. Opening it further, I found a set of keys that I recognized instantly. I had seen them dangling from the ignition in the Country Squire many times. Each key had a scrap of masking tape and a name.

"Ford"

"Office"

"Desk"

Big Joe Larson had left his whole business right here in the desk! I picked up the phone and called the number listed for Lou Sanders. He sounded sleepy.

"Yeah? Whadaya want? Who's this?"

"Ben Sherman over at the Home Reader Service. Big Joe is still gone and I'm wondering about getting paid."

"So am I. So what?"

"Do you have his phone number?"

"He calls *me*, kid. I ain't never called *him*."

"Are you coming back in here?" I asked.

"Not unless Big Joe Larson mysteriously reappears, which is less likely than the second coming of Jesus."

His coughing cut his laughter short. He abruptly hung up on me.

After staring at the blank wall for fifteen minutes, frustrated about not getting paid, I took out the checkbook and looked at it again. I put it back, but grabbed the set of keys and secured the door on my way out.

Big Joe's station wagon was full of gas. What a temptation! I locked it quickly and rode home on my bike.

Sleep was restless. Dreams of getting caught with Big Joe's keys woke me with a start several times. I got up and checked my dresser drawer. The keys were still there.

At noon the next day, I rode my bike back to Oak Park, unlocked the door to the offices and found the checkbook in the drawer. I took it across the street to the bank.

"Hello. My name is Ben Sherman. I work for the Home Reader Service across the street... right over there. Um... I do errands for Mr. Larson. He needs his balance."

The teller didn't blink. Taking a deposit slip from the checkbook, she wiggled in a tight skirt to a long drawer in the back. She handed back the slip on which she had written $7.06.

Back at the office, I looked through the letters in his desk, this time taking a better inventory. Big Joe owed me a week's pay. I had keys to the office, the desk, and the car. The bank account had nothing in it, but it remained open.

Again, I rode my bike back to school and returned to Oak Park at four. This was getting old, especially with the keys to the station wagon in my pocket. I unlocked the office door and turned on the lights.

As I was rummaging through the drawers again, a voice from behind startled me, "Mistah Larson here?" A small fellow of about sixty with a brown bald head and watery eyes looked like he'd been drinking since morning.

"No, sir. He's been called away."

"I'm George," he said in a raspy voice. "Building super. Here's his mail." He held several envelopes out to me. "He no come git his mail. Big Joe never miss his mail."

There were two windowed envelopes from The National Distributing House of Canton, Ohio.

"Rent's due. Big Joe never late. Never miss his mail. Never late on rent."

"How much is it?" I asked.

"He knows."

"Maybe I can find the check, if you tell me."

The diminutive man twisted his face. "I can't tell a boy. You jus' a boy. I dunno. "

He watched me rip opened the first envelope which contained a check made out to the Home Reader Service for a hundred and forty-four dollars.

"It's your choice," I said, opening the second.

"Okay. You straight up kid. Rent forty-eight."

"For the month?"

"Who pays that kinda rent? Big Joe pay forty-eight, twice a month. First and fifteenth."

The second envelope had a check for eighty dollars.

"Come in, Mister, uh...?"

"George."

"Come in, Mister George. I'll see if your check is here."

"Just George."

I went into Big Joe's office and got his checkbook. The envelope with old bank statements also had cancelled checks including several for forty-eight dollars made payable to Lark Investors. Each was dated either the first or the fifteenth of previous months. I placed a blank check over a cancelled one and carefully copied Big Joe's hand. He had a nondescript wiggly line for a signature. Too simple.

"Lark Investors?" I asked George as I handed him the check hoping the ink was dry.

"That's right!" he beamed, showing the first sign of brightness. "Big Joe never pay late!"

George hurried out the door and down the steps.

"Where do I pick up his mail?" I called behind him.

"Down here at Bloomberg's," he yelled from the bottom. "Postman don't climb no stairs."

I retuned to the checkbook, tore out a deposit slip, and wrote in the amounts of the two checks from National Distributing. My father had instructed me about bank matters when I took over the savings account my grandpa had opened for me at my birth. I printed "for deposit only" on the back of the checks and copied Joe's squiggly signature. I put the deposit in a Home Reader Service business envelope and ran it across the street to the outside deposit box.

We had everything here except Big Joe Larson. I called Mr. Sanders again. This time, he didn't try to disguise his grumpiness.

"Geez, kid, what the heck?"

"Sorry to bother you, but I know how we can get paid."

"Oh, for the love of Pete, you're a real pain in the neck. What're *you* gonna do?"

"Do you have more cards to collect on?"

"No, and Battle's out too."

"If I start the crew up again next Monday, can you come get our cards by the end of the week? By then, Big Joe will be back. We can't lose time while he's away."

"He ain't comin' back." Sanders assured me.

"Yes he is. I talked to him just now. Family emergency. He said he's in Vacaville."

"Vacaville? He called in?"

"Yep. Just got off the phone."

I wondered if there could be a medal for being the biggest liar in Sacramento.

"OK, fine. But, if I don't get cards, I don't get paid. This is horse pucky kid, if ya wanna know. Big Joe shoulda called me. I can't miss a week with nothin' comin' in."

"I know. Me neither. Thanks, Mr. Sanders. I'll see you next Friday."

"Yeah, right. I guess you'll see me Friday. I don't know why I'm doing this."

He hung up without signing off again.

I took the lists of names and the keys, locked the office door, and rode my bike home. That night, I asked my dad if you make a deposit on the same day you write a check, how does the bank know you have enough to pay for the check?

He explained bank hours.

"It all happens on a single bank day," he explained, "no matter what time you make your deposit or write your check. Why?"

"Just a math question."

I breathed my first sigh of relief. I rationalized, even though I might be fudging on signatures, I only wanted Big Joe's business to keep moving. I had grown attached to the regular paychecks and cash bonuses. Over the weekend, I called all seven of the other door-to-door guys, but only three could make it back on Monday, or *ever* for that matter. They either had other jobs already or their parents had forbidden them to return.

Frank Battle first asked who gave me his phone number. When I insisted Big Joe told me to call both closers, and that I had just talked to Mr. Sanders, he told me to leave him alone. He didn't mince words.

"Big Joe's a thousand miles from here. No matter what kind of bull you're spreading, I known Big Joe a long time. We've seen the last of him."

Hanging up on me had become contagious.

I had one closer and four boys. Not bad. I would start with half of Joe's business. On Monday, the three boys waited for me on the stairs as I peddled into the back lot.

"Where's Big Joe?"

"Are we working?"

"I gotta be home by seven."

I scurried up the stairs and unlocked the door.

"Wait for me at the car. I gotta pick up some cards."

"We're going out without Big Joe?"

"He's out of town on an emergency. Wait at the car!"

I tried a little too hard to use an authoritative tone, and my adolescent voice cracked. They looked suspicious and no one moved toward the station wagon. I went in and picked up some survey cards and a map of the suburbs.

There is nothing like sitting behind the wheel at fourteen. What a rush. I should have been out of my mind with excitement, but I thought only of the trouble I faced if anything happened to the car or its passengers. I didn't drive over the speed limit. The guys were statues all the way out to East Sacramento. Nobody asked for the radio as they usually did. Nobody talked about girls or football. They knew something unfathomably wrong had to be happening.

"So look," I began, facing straight ahead, "we're going to keep working until Mr. Larson comes back. Our paychecks are due this Friday. If we don't get paid, we can all quit. Till then, we gotta keep the cards rolling in."

"So, you haven't heard from him?"

I didn't answer. Instead, I asked the guy beside me to hand out some copies of a new spiel I'd been working on over the weekend and had laboriously typed in four individual copies. My first attempt at a typewriter showed numerous strike-outs. The boys read to themselves.

"Can you memorize that in about fifteen minutes?"

"Are we really going to say this?" one asked.

"This is selling magazines, not taking surveys," another added.

"Man," said the third, "this sounds like the truth!"

"I know. Promise me you won't tell. Let's just see what happens if we do it straight."

"Why not?" the guy in the front seat asked. "I'm in! I never liked that mountain camp stuff, anyway."

Rancho Cordova looked welcoming. I dropped the guys off at a corner and gave them several blocks to canvas, telling them I'd pick them up an hour later.

At first, I sat in the car trembling. What could I be thinking? I had passed two patrol cars on the way out of town, and my hands were shaking all the way up to my shoulders. Why change the spiel? What if they all came back empty-handed? What about permits? That's what got us in trouble in Roseville.

I saw my partner coming down the walk from his first house. He waved a card at me, smiling. Wow! I jumped out of the car to hit the doors on the other side of the street. That would help reduce my jitters.

We were back to the office by half-past seven, later than we'd ever been. But, I had driven like an old lady and we had to stop to call one of the parents. The guys talked all the way back, giving details about how their new spiel worked, how they had each changed the approach a bit to make it more personal and even more truthful.

We worked Rancho Cordova for a week. Cards came in slowly on Monday and Tuesday, but we improved as we became more familiar with our new pitch. On Friday, we brought in forty cards. Lou waited on the stoop when we returned. He followed me up to the office and I handed him just over a hundred cards for the week.

"Holy Samolies, kid!" he said. "This'll keep me going. How'd you do this with just four guys?"

"I changed the spiel some," I explained. "These people know they're buying magazines, and we told them we'd give them a week to decide before signing an official agreement."

"You what?" Lou asked, dismayed. He fell into a wood chair staring at me in disbelief.

"Notice the day on the top of each. I wrote that so you would show up exactly a week later as we said."

"Huh?" Lou seemed utterly confused.

"We're being truthful with them. We hit a lot more houses because people say no earlier in the spiel."

"We also suggested they talk it over with their husbands. We dropped the camp thing and added that we wouldn't get paid if they decided against it, but we didn't want that to pressure them. We said we only want happy customers."

"Say again ..."

"I said we only want... "

"No. Don't tell me again."

"Lou, we've got over a hundred signatures here and they all know they're buying magazines – at least, until the old man comes home."

"I know. I know. I hear ya. Let me think a minute."

He waved his hands in the air and put them both over his face. He looked like he might explode. After a while he began slowly constructing how he would change his pitch.

"I can use that part about you kids not getting paid, and innocent boys earning money for, uh, for what?"

"For college, Lou. It's never too early to start saving."

"That'll work. That's as good as anything, I guess." Sanders puffed out his bottom lip in mock sadness, "I really liked the camp in the mountains thing, though."

We agreed to try it for another week.

"If Big Joe calls in here, you tell him to call me pronto, y'hear?"

"Of course," I said. "I told him that last time."

"I think he's got you buffaloed, kid," Sanders said. "But who cares? If I get contracts for these, I get paid with or without Big Joe."

"How's Mister Larson, son?" my dad asked at dinner.

"It's like he's not even there."

Anyone could interpret the truth from that statement.

"Well, you keep an eye on him. I couldn't find anything about Joe Larson as far as criminal records, but he sure acted strange not showing up to bail you boys out of trouble."

"I'm not really in a position to ask."

"True. Mind your own business, and do your work."

"Exactly," I said, smiling on the inside while I tried to furl my brow and look serious.

The office rent was paid and no other bills arrived. I needed to figure out payroll. On Saturday, back at the office, I lined up all the old cancelled checks on the desk. We all worked the same hours, but Big Joe had paid us differently. It took all my math skills to figure it out, but it looked like Joe paid me a bonus of fifty-cents for every card over thirty-five per week. I checked my formula with other paychecks and it worked.

I wrote three checks to cover the two week pay period plus bonuses. I carefully spelled each boy's name correctly and squiggled Big Joe's signature.

Lou Sanders said he would call me each day at four to tell me how that day's sales went, and we'd decide whether to continue or quit. Meanwhile, the boys were paid and they each committed to work with me for at least two more weeks. I didn't pay myself anything as I thought this certainly had to be against the law. However, I figured Joe would make it right if he returned, or I would soon figure out something else.

There were no cancelled checks for Mr. Sanders or Mr. Battle, so I had to ask.

"Lou, how much do you get paid?"

"None of your business. I get my checks from National just like Big Joe."

"Sorry," I said. "I didn't know."

Little did he suspect that I only wanted to make it right with him. This news couldn't be better. I only had to pay my three buddies out of the Home Reader Service account. Everything else was profit.

Checks arrived from National Distributors every week, and I made deposits in the outside bank box to avoid suspicion. Every second Friday, I paid the guys. As the bank account began to swell, and I had gone two months without any money for myself. On my fifteenth birthday, I decided to treat myself and make a withdrawal. I accurately calculated my pay and bonuses at the same rate and made out a check to myself to cover all my missed pay. As I deposited over three hundred dollars in my own savings account, my heart pounded like a bank robber.

I paid the landlord George monthly instead of semi-monthly to keep him from snooping. Lou gave up the daily phone calls and only came in briefly on Fridays. He always appeared to be looking over his shoulder as he picked up our cards and left in a hurry. I used his tally sheet to compare his numbers with the checks from National. They were never off a penny. Sanders didn't once mention Big Joe's absence, but he sure didn't seem comfortable.

I changed the bonuses to one dollar for every subscription contracted by Lou. The guys stayed a little longer at each house, and I had to remind them to move on if things weren't going well immediately. Our rides to the neighborhoods became upbeat cheering matches to get us pumped for a day of sales. The radio blasted again, and the guys were on fire when they hit the streets.

The same three guys worked with me through the spring, summer, fall and winter. We worked consistently five days a week and sometimes on a Saturday morning when everyone felt a little greedy. I targeted more upscale neighborhoods as we changed our spiel to sell subscriptions as Christmas gifts. In our second spring, we hit every downtown doctor and dentist office with amazing results. Each guy doubled his sales. Lou loved it as he could park his car and close a dozen sales walking a solid block of professional suites.

After eight months of working at the Home Reader Service without Big Joe, in October I received my driving learner's permit. The first time my mom took me for a drive in a parking lot, I threw our family car into gear and stomped on the accelerator sending her into a nervous fit.

"Stop! Start slower!" she pleaded. "This is a large dangerous machine. You must be more careful."

When I whipped out of the parking lot onto the busy streets, gave proper hand-signals, and even turned left against traffic at intersections, the poor woman didn't know what to say. Her driving lessons became limited to sucking wind through her teeth when she feared disaster.

"You are a very natural driver," she finally admitted.

In April, I passed my driving test with flying colors. I began driving the station wagon to and from work, secretly parking it at the supermarket a block from my house. A couple of my friends saw me driving one day and asked where I got the car.

"My boss," I explained.

None of us mentioned Big Joe again. The end of school approached, and I asked the guys about working through another summer. They each declined, having had their fill of soliciting. I too had become weary. I asked Lou what he'd do if we just closed down the Home Reader Service. He said he'd throw us boys a party and have another job in a week.

On my last day of tenth grade, Lou bought everybody pizza from the brand new Shakey's on the corner. I wrote the guys' checks and gave George notice that this would be our final month's rent. By then, I had run the Home Reader Service for almost two years.

Lou Sanders worked another few weeks before he had run through all our cards. Because it was summer vacation, I went along with him and learned about closing sales. He liked having a chauffeur and he chatted constantly. He'd had many jobs selling, advertising, starting his own distributing company, and he shared the ins and outs, ups and downs of each. I loved any excuse to sit behind the wheel of Big Joe's station wagon.

For several weeks after Lou sent off his final subscription form and I had turned in the office keys to George, I continued to check the mail at Bloomberg's. What a great summer job, driving over to Oak Park once a day in my secret car to check the mail. The payments from National dribbled in as Lou's orders cleared.

Finally, the checks stopped. Lou's list indicated that we were finished. Leaving the original seven dollars and six cents in the Home Reader Service bank account, I withdrew fourteen hundred and change.

As my last act in the role of self-appointed interim manager, I put my bicycle in the back of the station wagon, drove it over to Lou's house and left the keys in his mailbox. I rode my bike home, beaming all the way.

Sweardagod.

Warehouse

About two dozen guys lived with me in the dorms during the summer of '66. We looked like a bunch of bums, wearing Salvation Army clothes, giving each other buzz cuts with a worn-out barber's electric shaver, washing our clothes only after they could stand up by themselves. We were trying to earn and save enough to pay tuition in fall. Mac had a job life-guarding at a Navy base in Long Beach. Alan drove a summer school bus for the Anaheim School District. Billy, Sam and Gibb spread tar every day for a roof sealing company. They had to leave their stinking clothes on the lawn each night.

I had three paltry jobs − making sandwiches at a tiny lunch place, washing dishes at a family restaurant, and driving a delivery truck for a furniture company − all three for a buck thirty-five an hour.

The college cafeteria was closed during summer, nobody could afford to eat out, and there weren't any kitchens in our dorm. On days I didn't work at the food places, a normal meal might be a loaf of bread and ten slices of bologna between five of us. With no refrigerators in our rooms, we had to finish off anything perishable in one sitting. Communal food sharing became the norm, without any mayonnaise.

Then, I learned to cook fried rice. Every year, a rice farmer friend of my parents' would bring them a huge supply of brown rice. One day every autumn, they'd come home and there would be another ten-pound sack on their porch. Since the rice had begun to take over their garage, I brought a huge supply back to college.

For a buck apiece at the Goodwill, I bought a hotplate, an electric frying pan, and a saucepan. While cutting meat for sandwiches during my day job, I saved the unused shavings in a paper bag. Each night, I came home with a couple of pounds of pastrami, beef, ham, corned beef and turkey. With the meat sizzling in the electric frying pan, I boiled three cups of rice with six cups of water in the saucepan. Once cooked, I poured the whole batch on top of the meat and let it simmer.

Every night, we ate sitting on the second floor corridor outside my room watching the colors of the setting sun through the smog. These are my best college memories – balmy Southern California evenings when classes weren't in session – sitting with a bunch of chums whose bellies I kept full.

About four weeks into summer, Mrs. Hagood called me from the Career Center.

"Anybody over there looking for work?"

"Whatcha got?" I replied, always looking for something better than minimum wage.

She usually had a dishwashing or busboy job at a local restaurant. One time, my neighbor and I responded immediately to a gig as models for a life-drawing class that promised us three bucks an hour. We stayed three minutes, however, when we learned what we would *not* be wearing.

"This one's a winner," she assured me. "Thrifty Warehouse. They've need strike replacements. It's about four miles from campus over in east Anaheim."

Coming from a professional family where both my mom and dad never belonged to a union, I didn't have any

160

feelings one way or another about a labor dispute. It sounded like somebody else's problem.

"Any guys over there looking for work?" she asked again, not waiting for me to respond. "They need as many bodies as you can get. Six A.M. Monday morning. Don't be late. Come by my office tomorrow. I'll give you the letter with their address and contact information."

"Yes, ma'am. Six o'clock on Monday morning, as many as I can find. What's the pay?"

"Three-fourteen an hour, same as their starting union wages."

I couldn't even imagine that kind of money, over twice the minimum wage. My voice went up an octave. "We'll *be* there!"

By Sunday, I had found four willing guys. Mac liked life-guarding but hated the commute to Long Beach that took him three bus transfers. Alan got about the same pay driving for the school district, so he declined. The three tar babies said they liked doing roofs, but I suspected that they had some feelings about not breaking a union strike. They asked a lot of questions before turning me down.

Two guys who lived in an apartment near the campus and hung around the dorms said they were up for it as they both worked for lousy wages and short hours at restaurants. The four of us crowded into the front seat of my '49 Chevy pickup and arrived at about fifteen before six Monday morning.

The warehouse nestled itself into a cluster of industrial buildings that were new to the area. Rows of cement structures with tin roofs had replaced the orange groves that once divided small towns. During my college years, the orchards of Orange County disappeared. Construction connected cities into one massive parking lot. It should be renamed Concrete County.

A tall thin guy in a half-tucked white shirt met us inside the door. "Is this all of you?" I told him I could get more

161

guys. He looked over my shoulder at the parking lot outside. "Good, the picketers aren't here yet. Come on in boys. How many more can you get? I can use at least two dozen. You know anybody?"

"Sure. We just want to work a day first so we can tell people."

"Call me Larry. Just Larry," he loosened his tie and rotated his head on his neck. "The work is steady, not hard. It's repetitive, not monotonous. It can get heavy, but it ain't back-breaking. Can everybody here lift fifty pounds?" he asked.

We all nodded.

"Well, let's see what we can get done!"

He walked down a wide aisle to the back of the long warehouse. The aisles separated rows of shelves thirty feet high. Boxes on the bottom of the front rows were open.

"Basically, you shop for the stores here," Just Larry explained. "You will be pickers." We arrived at dozens of clipboards hanging from nails. "Basically, you take one of these," he held up a board, "and, you grab a stack of totes." He picked up plastic boxes with wire handles. "... and put 'em on a cart there." He put the empties on a flatbed cart. "Basically, you find the items on the order," he smacked the clipboard with his open palm, "...out there." He pointed with a flourish to a sea of racks extending the width and breadth of the warehouse. "You pick the orders by putting each store's items in the totes. It's basically pretty basic. The totes go on those bottom conveyor belts. Empty boxes go on the top belts. Think you can handle it?"

More nodding.

"Basically, just be sure not to mix stores, and don't mix totes with empties."

We looked at Just Larry.

"Well, go ahead. We're burning daylight."

Instructions over. Training complete.

162

Mac said, "Let's go boys. Sounds *basically pretty basic* to me."

"That's the spirit," Just Larry beamed.

Each of us grabbed a clipboard that matched the name of a store. Each page had a list of items, quantity, aisle and row. Each board had tote labels with the appropriate store number. On the back of the board, there was a warehouse map. One conveyor for product, the other for empties. What could be simpler?

It didn't take long to get the hang of filling orders. In a half hour, I completed my first page, stuck a label on the tote, and plopped in on the conveyor. Just Larry interrupted my progress.

"They're pickers," he explained. "You're gonna be a loader.

He walked me to the front of the warehouse where we had come in.

"Take the totes off and stack them according to the store number on the pallets by the truck loading doors." He pointed at garage doors running across the front of the building. "Just be sure that the right tote gets on the right pallet. Stack them six high, no higher. It shouldn't be too hard for a while. One loader can usually stay ahead of ten pickers. Later, some of the supervisors are coming in. When they start picking, you'll be hopping."

"What if ...?"

"Don't worry about it. I will be going back and forth. If I see your lines getting full, I'll jump in to help for awhile. Or, I'll find somebody."

At eleven, a horn sounded and Just Larry motioned for us to gather at the front. He explained that there were about a hundred picketers carrying signs out on the street in front of the gates.

"I ordered lunch for you. We can all eat inside. Avoid confrontation," he explained.

Upstairs in an employee lunchroom, there were Kentucky Fried Chicken boxes full of bread, mashed potatoes, gravy and chicken. We must have looked starved that first day. We ate everything but the napkins.

The four of us worked till six, twelve hours with a half-hour for lunch and three short ten-minute breaks. Fortunately, we were all young and had bodies like spring steel. But, even my soccer-trained legs began cramping around four o'clock.

I only had brief glimpses of my compatriots all day. They kept up with the supervisors pretty easily. After lunch, the boxes came in steadily. Just Larry added another loader to help me in front. By six, my whole body yakked at me every time I lifted another tote. As the conveyors shut off and we gathered in the front to go home, the six supervisors prepared to load my pallets into trucks and drive to the area stores. Their day had just begun. The truck drivers had honored the warehousemen's strike. My heart wanted to volunteer to stay and help, but my body absolutely forbade me to step forward.

Just Larry said we'd get checks each Friday. He calculated that we'd earned $43.96 that first day, eight hours plus four overtime. Not only had he bought our lunch, he'd paid us while we were eating.

A whole week's pay at the restaurant earned me thirty-nine bucks before deductions. I figured that this strike-breaking might be the best thing since blue jeans.

Monday night, hearing about our pay, the three roofers agreed to give the warehouse a try. Mac and I knocked on every door in our dorm and came up with more willing bodies, and the two off-campus guys said they'd bring some friends. Tuesday morning, we had seventeen workers. Alan drove us to the warehouse in the school bus before his shift.

Tuition for a whole semester at Chapman College in 1966 was $550. Larry gave me a check for $219 on Friday. He also promised me foreman's pay if the strike continued

164

and I kept over fifteen on the crew. I told him that I had worked a deal with my guys to drive them safely to and from work and feed them lunch, if they'd agree to work for three bucks an hour.

"Three fourteen," he said, correcting me.

"They're going to give me the fourteen cents," I said.

"No kidding? How did you come up with that idea?"

"Three bucks is more than enough. They've never seen that kind of money. I have a buddy with a school bus, and I gotta give him something for gas and his time. None of these guys have cars. It's worth it to them."

"You ought to be in management," he beamed.

Larry liked my transportation idea as it got us all through the gates at one time. This minimized his security worries. Plus, he didn't think any of the strikers would harm a school bus. If my boys agreed, he said, he'd take care of it by transferring the fourteen cents an hour difference directly to my paycheck, rather than have me collect from them individually.

"There really aren't many rules running a distribution house during a work stoppage," he explained. "But, I need paper from each guy releasing the fourteen cents."

Hearing about three bucks an hour plus overtime, guys knocked on my door all week.

"Is it true? You're making three bucks an hour?"

"It's three fourteen, but you're giving me the fourteen cents to get you there and back through the picket lines, plus the warehouse buys you lunch," I told each guy.

Nobody flinched. I had them sign a slip of paper that authorized Thrifty to transfer fourteen cents an hours from their paycheck to mine. I also had them write down their name, address, and social security number so there'd be no mistake and signing in would go quicker when they got to work.

My room turned into an employment office. By the following Monday, we had a full bus.

My hourly wage skyrocketed. I earned $3.65 as a
foreman, plus an additional $6.16 per hour based on forty-
two guys at fourteen cents apiece. I took out a scrap of paper
and multiplied $9.81 times 40 hours. We all got time and a
half overtime for four hours every day which lifted my
hourly wage to $14.72 for the remaining twenty hours per
week. My next Friday check would be about $686 gross.
After deductions, in one week, I'd have fall semester tuition.
In another week, I'd have room and board. Unbelievable.

I paid Alan ten bucks a day to drive us about seven
miles roundtrip to and from the warehouse. Just to put this
in perspective, even with all my part time jobs, I lived on
less than twenty dollars a month. All of us did. The college
got the rest.

Just Larry ran our short crew without any help from me,
even though he paid me foreman's wages. He took me off
the loading area and assigned me to a simple job running the
cardboard compactor. A second set of conveyors carried
empty boxes from the picking aisles to a machine that
pressed them into a giant cube. Twice a day, I pushed a
button on the compactor, waited a minute, then removed the
compressed block of cardboard. A supervisor driving a fork
lift carried the cubes to the rear of the building where they
were loaded into a waiting trailer.

Larry thought he did me a favor, but I didn't really like
having a boring job. I passed my time cleaning up the
compactor room, helped with the pallets on the loading
dock, and sometimes wandered around checking in with my
guys. Some of them seemed like potential loose canons
known for getting into trouble, but they couldn't distract
each other much. The work kept them very busy and
isolated.

If anybody screwed up, came late, or missed a day, I
replaced him with somebody else who had heard about the
three bucks an hour. We lost a few guys the first week, but
thereafter settled into the same crew working six to six

166

Monday through Friday. Nobody complained. In the morning, we weren't awake enough to speak and we almost fell asleep exhausted on the short ride home. We came in before the strikers arrived and left after they had gone home.

On the third Wednesday, I hit the bed hard as soon as I got back to the dorm. A loud knock on the door shook me out of a deep sleep. At first, I thought I had overslept when my bleary eyes read eight-thirty on my alarm clock. Groggy, it came to me that somebody had knocked. I opened the door and saw that the shadows were long as the sun hung low in the western sky. Relieved it was still evening, I tried to focus on two men who obscured most of the doorframe. Dressed nicely in slacks and pressed shirts, they were both in their forties and looked like weight-lifters.

"Mr. Sherman?" one asked.

"Huh?"

I almost turned around to see if my father stood behind me. Nobody called me that.

"May we come in?"

They weren't small. One black, one brown, they didn't seem to want to wait long outside. Each one leaned into my room and surveyed my quarters.

"I'll come out," I said, not feeling comfortable until I found out who they were.

The larger of the two, a man with bulging eyes and a soft voice, stepped into my room as the other closed the door to wait outside.

"We're from the union," he almost whispered.

"Sir?" I tried to look around his large frame at my closed door.

"No problem," he assured me. "I wanna talk without bein' disturbed."

"Okay," I said, moving to my desk to pull out a chair for him.

I'd feel better to have him sitting down and not towering over me. I sat on the edge of my bed, preparing to make a lot of noise right here at the end of my life. He thanked me politely and sat with no concern about my nervousness.

"You boys are making your way through this college," he began. "I respect that. I got a son over at Long Beach State right now. He's doin' real good bein' he's the first in our family t'go t'college."

He stopped to gather his thoughts.

"My wife don't work. She's got three youngins' to tend."

His hands and forearms showed that he worked hard for a living. His shoulders looked like foam football pads. His large head sat on a neck the size of my thigh. The silky lilt that is often present in a mature black man's voice floated out and filled the room, as if he would break into singing soft blues at any moment.

"Our union has asked me t'come over here and talk t'you 'bout this strike."

"Sir...uh?"

"Lemme finish," he more begged than demanded. "I gotta get it all out or I'll forget somethin'. Just hang on a second."

He wiped his mouth with his open palm and it came to me that he might be more nervous than I.

"Y'all been doing good work over there. We got some people inside who been reporting that you just college kids. Y'all don' know nothin' 'bout unions and management, 'bout labor contracts."

I nodded. "Good pay for hard work," I said.

"Right," he continued. "Hell, I don't know much more'n y'all. But, the basic fact right here is that y'all's workin' is keepin' this strike goin' longer than we can afford."

He took a deep breath. His brow furled and his lips began forming around words before he could say them.

168

"You the one our inside guys say to contact. You the one got all these guys workin'." He nodded his head at me. "Right?"

I returned his motion. Words weren't going to come easily. My main concern at the moment had to do with not peeing in my pants.

"We'd like to offer you a deal."

He waited for me to say something, but had to content himself with mere nodding.

"We'd like you to slow down the process from the inside, and we'll make it worth your while."

He had my attention.

"Nothin' fancy, just a minor mishap here 'n there. Nothin' t'git you in trouble, understand? Just something to tip this in our favor. We know they're barely getting' the product out. We know the stores are plenty upset and they want this to be over. We just need a little help from inside, and it needs to come from you college kids. We don't want nobody hurt. That's important. We like them guys in there. This union thing's bigger 'n just us, or just this here warehouse. People bigger n'me are watchin' what happens down here. It's not good, understand? It's scary for me too. But, we gotta do somethin' to get this thing over so's we can all go back to work."

Whatever thoughts came, there were no actual words. I'm sure my face gave me away. He seemed satisfied.

"You think on it. I don't wanna come back here. And you shore don't want nobody else comin' to visit ya."

He turned and went out the door closing it quietly behind him. Obviously, he'd said what he had come to say and he wanted to get out of there.

I sat on my bed shaking for several minutes. I went to the closed blinds to peek out. The two men were gone. I opened the door and saw no one on the second floor or in the parking lot.

I didn't tell anybody.

We all filed onto the bus the next morning, but nothing felt the same to me. I hadn't slept well, continually thinking about the visit. The fantastic money I earned seemed to pale when reflected in the face of the polite worker with a son like me in college. And, he had made it clear that the next visit would not be from him, and would not be pleasant.

About ten that morning, my trash compactor froze halfway through its cycle. Nothing seemed to be jammed. I tried clearing what I could, to no avail. I called Just Larry and he brought with him a couple of blue-suited maintenance guys.

"Mechanical?" muttered one.

"Mmm, hmmm," agreed the other.

"Beyond us," the first told the boss.

They stood around waiting for an outside repairman most of the morning. The cardboard conveyors still ran, dumping boxes into the compactor. Just Larry climbed up a ladder and closed the gate so empty boxes continued to make their circular route around the warehouse. By three, when the repairman finally arrived, there were boxes filling the belts above everyone's heads and they were beginning to drop out into the aisles between the stacks of merchandise. It amazed me how rapidly the entire warehouse reacted to one flaw in the process. The belts had to be stopped. Larry's voice boomed out of the loudspeakers.

"Shutting down early, folks. No overtime today. See you all tomorrow at six."

When I got home, I found an envelope with no address slid under my door. Inside, I found ten five-dollar bills.

Sweardagod.

Tuesday morning, the compactor had been repaired. All of the totes were gone from the loading area, and there were no trucks outside. The supervisors had been up all night again, and now they were driving deliveries. The cardboard conveyors cranked up promptly at six and the warehouse hummed along as before.

My guys became more proficient at filling orders each day. The returns were minimal as accuracy increased. Enthused by typical college-guy competition, they invented contests and pooled money to determine the fastest and most accurate picker. Productivity skyrocketed. Just Larry assigned two more loaders to get pallets into trucks and make room for store orders that arrived more rapidly from the aisles. I had to run the compactor more often and a driver stayed busy carting my cubes to the back lot. This is how the warehouse ran normally, with every station, every position, every function interconnected, like the legs on a giant centipede.

At four-thirty on Thursday, right after our afternoon break, the fire alarms went off. Ordered outside, we stood and waited while firemen came and inspected the building. It turned out to be a faulty sensor in an area where none of us worked, much to my relief. Just Larry had to call off the order selectors while his regular staff made safety checks and reports for the fire marshal. We all went home early again.

Coming back from a movie that evening, I found another envelope on the floor inside my door. It contained another fifty dollars.

Early the next day, our fifth Friday, the union voted in favor of a new offer from management. News spread fast. The regular workers would return Monday and our services were no longer required. My crew worked right up until six when Just Larry walked with us out to our bus. As we boarded, he eagerly shook our hands, wished us luck in school, and thanked each guy personally.

We drove through the gates for our last time. The big school bus turned onto the boulevard, and we passed dozens of union members on our left who were picking up signs and chairs and some debris along the street. They stopped to wave as we drove by. We were all sinking down in our seats as we weren't used to seeing the picketers, but Alan honked the horn and the people on the street cheered and applauded. This stunned us. For five weeks, we came early and stayed late, ate our lunches inside, all so we'd never confront the angry mob of strikers.

"Maybe they're just happy it's over," I wondered out loud.

"Or really happy to see us go," Mac added behind me.

After we got off the bus, as Alan swung it around in the dormitory parking lot, we saw why the picketers had cheered. On the driver's side of the bus, where we couldn't see when we boarded, Alan had taped a long banner with tall painted letters that said, *"Thanks for 42 tuitions!"*

Thrifty paid us another way as well. The experience provided us a profound incentive to stay in college.

Pranks

College life went through significant social transformations in the late Sixties. Regrettably, I attended in the <u>early</u> Sixties. Life on campus was still pretty stiff when I got there. Staff and faculty took responsibility for our parenting as well as our educational growth. Something called "in loco parentis" just meant too much control. Conversely, our choice to leave home to go away to college had more to do with freedom and mobility than schooling and intellectual preparation. Later in the Sixties, this created a tension between the generations that finally exploded onto the streets. Meanwhile, in 1964, freshmen had rules. Strict rules. As usual, prior to the Women's Movement, the rules were for the girls, not the boys. Pardon my politically incorrect language, but this was the way it was written:

- *Freshmen girls must be in the dormitory by seven-thirty for the first six weeks, and by ten on weekends.*
- *If you maintain a spotless record, after week four, you may stay out till nine on weeknights.*
- *Starting in your sophomore year, the weekend curfew will be extended to midnight.*
- *Privileges will be revoked if a girl comes in late.*

Boys had dorms with exterior corridors and we had no hours. They figured that if they locked up the girls, the boys wouldn't get into mischief. That was a miscalculation.

We squirmed in class, but it didn't take a freshman long to learn that obedience and attendance significantly affected grades. We pretended to be engaged in class. To exercise freedom, we waited till we got back to the dorms. Pity the housing staff. They negotiated a skinny path between their quest for order and our need to scatter wild oats.

Practical jokes were one of the tamer ways of letting off steam and sharing some great laughs. We called them "Ratfinking." In prison movie lingo, a ratfink tattled on people. Also called a stoolie or stooge, he deserved retribution, so the inmates came up with public embarrassment to punish the offender. The perpetrators remained anonymous. Somehow, this transferred to our practical jokes in the Sixties.

Often directed at some perceived injustice, or just to add a little action to our lives, we instigated a run of public jokes that became legendary. Every semester we held a private ceremony in which we crowned the RF King by pouring a bottle of cheap beer over his head. I held the title four semesters in a row.

Elsewhere, RFs took on greater proportions than ours. At USC, pre-law students slanted elections by distributing ranting letters over the signature of an opponent – a technique borrowed later by some of the same "political tricksters" in national presidential campaigns. At Cal Berkely, fraternity boys superimposed a rival's face onto another photograph showing him in a compromising position. They posted hundreds of copies around campus, in stairwells, restroom stalls and library cubicles. They used "college pranks" as their excuse when later caught and questioned.

Other imaginative jokes include the famous MIT balloon that blew up from underground in the middle of the annual football game between Army and Navy. One year, Cal Poly nerds hacked into the UCLA computer that prepared their half-time cards, and the unsuspecting Bruins spelled out "Go Poly" across their cheering section.

Following are the award-winning misdeeds performed at my college, Chapman University, in a brief period between 1964 and 1967. I'm happy to say that none of these affected elections, got anybody arrested, permanently hurt reputations, exposed improprieties, or damaged property.

As years passed, a few stories remained in the folklore with embellishments, retold enough times to approach mythical status. Some others have disappeared forever.

These are definitely male stories. In a world filled with chick flicks and relationship novels, it's hard to find male entertainment that isn't filled with brutality or explosions. That's really too bad. I had great fun being a guy in college. We were playful and irreverent at times, but never violent.

Rusty

When freshman girls emerged from their first four weeks of seclusion, the sight of forbidden fruit gave our upperclassmen a feral appetite. We freshman predators didn't stand a chance. Here we were in college, away from home, with no hours or restrictions, hormones raging, all ready to rock and roll, with no dance partners. The older guys had jobs, which meant cars and cash.

We often obsessed on how poorly we were doing on the dating scene.

"These chicks are impossible," Wayne moaned.

"They'll come around next semester," our sophomore mentor, Mac, assured us.

"Like, I can wait another semester," Mike pined. "It's been a dry two months."

"Pisses me off," Bob added. "They're aloof, unapproachable. I strike up a conversation, and it always turns to what kind of car I drive."

"I know. My cherry Impala is sitting at home. Why can't freshman have cars?"

"They even flirt with professors," Mike added. "And, their grades show it."

"They make me puke."

"I have sworn off. Completely."

"OK, let's look elsewhere," I suggested. "We've wasted our time chasing lame dates for half a semester."

"What dates? You've had dates?"

"Coffee? Study break? You call that a date?"

"If a girl stays to talk to me after all the food is gone on her tray, I consider that a major score."

"Martha told me to shut up in the library yesterday. That's cool, right?"

"OK. Obviously, none of us are getting anywhere," I said. "Maybe we're looking the wrong direction."

"Huh?"

"Look across the street," I said.

Right across the street from our dorm, you could see the mascot's name painted across the façade of the local high school gymnasium.

"Think back just a few months ago. Who were we losing our girlfriends to?"

No response.

"High school? Our senior year? Remember? It wasn't that long ago. Didn't the girls go crazy for college guys?"

"Now that you mention it, some of them did," Wayne said.

"There are girls over there who look at us a lot differently than the freshmen girls here do."

"Stands to reason."

"Uh huh. And, they're eighteen."

"Legal."

"How do we meet them?" Bob asked.

"The high school doesn't allow college students on their property," Mac told us. "Nice idea, but no trespassing."

"Let's enroll," I suggested.

"What?"

"Are you nuts?"

"In high school?"

"We can do it!" I insisted.

Pacing back and forth in my dorm room while the others followed me with their eyes, I let some temporary genius roll.

"I can go over there and register like I'm a transferring senior. The school year is already going. I can doctor up my transcript from high school."

"How are you going to do that?" Mike asked.

"Just blank out the last semester and change the date on the top. The student newspaper office has a copier."

"And you'll introduce us to chicks?"

"You're nuts," Wayne repeated.

"Go on. Let him finish," Mac said, now more interested.

"I'll say my Dad got transferred here and we had to move," I went on.

"Say he's in the Marines at El Toro."

"What's your address? You'll need an address."

"How much is a downtown post office box?" I asked.

"A buck fifty a month," Mac said.

"You're renting and looking for a house. You'll have a permanent address soon."

"Sure, the P.O. box is temporary."

"Good idea for a day or two," Mike said. But how are you going to go to high school and college at the same time?"

"Let's look at our schedules. I won't go alone," I suggested.

"Huh?"

"If I fake a high school transcript, I can enroll making it look like I only need four classes for a few weeks to graduate at mid year. We can split up the classes."

"We'll all go?"

"Bull!"

"No way!"

"You *are* nuts!" Mike said. Wayne and Bob nodded.

"Brilliant!" Mac exclaimed. "And that way you *all* meet girls. That was your intention in the first place. The high school is a big place. They'll never know."

The guys rethought their first reaction.

179

"Yes!" I said. "This is do-able. If we're caught, what law have we broken? We'll just call it an RF."

"Or a class project," Bob suggested. "We could say we did it to write a paper on high school life. I need to come up with something for my English term paper."

"Anyway, we can try it, right?"

We looked at our class schedules and found we had enough variance that the four of us could cover four classes from nine to three, Monday through Friday.

The next morning, I enrolled at the high school. We settled on calling ourselves Rusty Gibbs, the combined names of Wayne's dog and Bob's hamster. It was a lot easier than any of us expected. The school required only one form filled out by a parent. Mac did a nice job of signing for Rusty's dad, Mr. Gibbs.

Starting the next Monday, I showed up for second period U.S. History at nine. I had to hustle from my eight o'clock college English class that ended promptly ten minutes before the hour. Mike attended Calculus at ten. We had a free fourth period and a lunch for fifth. We picked classes in which each of us could use some repeat work. Wayne did English at one. Bob went to Physiology at two.

Our original scheme had been to meet girls, but our advantage as college guys disappeared when we enrolled as a high school senior.

"Oops. We didn't think of that."

To our distinct advantage, however, there's always something intriguing about the "new guy." By the second week, we each dated a girl from the class we attended. To assure that the four different girls didn't find out they were dating the same guy, we each came up with a different nickname, saying that we hated the name Rusty. Socially, four guys were new at school. Officially, the school enrolled only one Rusty Gibbs. In December, we completed our finals and got straight B's on our report card. Our attendance wasn't consistent, but our tests scores were stellar. With these final requirements met, the high school issued Rusty a diploma. As they had no mid-year commencement, he would graduate with the other seniors in spring.

We told the student yearbook editor about our scam and he offered the final touch. He added a picture of Rusty after the final deadline so that no one would catch the joke. Right before our classes ended in spring, our own college student newspaper ran a copy of a page from the high school's yearbook showing a cocker spaniel's picture over the name Rusty Gibbs.

Sweardagod.

The boys poured a bottle of Rainier Ale over my head, anointing me the new RF King. Thus commenced my reign.

Bug

Already thinking about his morning classes, Mr. Doetkott, our new Residence Director, walked out the front door of his dorm apartment and reached for his keys to unlock his car. He couldn't believe what he saw. Furniture from the residence hall lounge sat in the reserved parking space instead of his VW Bug.

Doetkott had no time to look for his car, or even call the police, as he taught a class in five minutes. Known to be strict on tardiness, he jogged two blocks from the dorms to the campus, carrying his heavy briefcase. During the break between classes, he called his wife.

"I know," she said. "It's sitting in the lounge."

"My car?" he asked. "How did it get in the lounge?"

"Well, dear, I'm sure I didn't park it there."

"Dang those kids!" he said, "We've been RF'd."

"R what?" she asked.

"They don't like my reserved parking space. I'll handle it. Just get it out."

"I tried. It won't fit between the doors."

"Of course it will," he said. "They didn't take it apart to get it in there."

"Honey," his wife pleaded, "you're going to have to deal with this. I have school in twenty minutes, and my ride is here."

"Fine," he said, grumbling expletives under his breath as he ran off to his next class.

Surveying the "Bug in the Lobby Caper" later, Doetkott opened the sliding doors all the way and pushed his VW toward the opening. No way. The bumpers extended past the glass at least six inches on each side. He pulled the car back to investigate the opening. Even removing the glass door wouldn't gain him the room he needed on either side.

Henry, the math wiz, drifted in and surveyed the situation.

"Gotta problem?" he asked Mr. Doetkott.

"No. I brought it in here to wax it."

"Other people pushed it in here," the wise student commented.

"Of course they did! Did you see them? Did you see who?"

"They picked up one side and angled it in."

"Did you see them do that?" Doetkott asked.

"No. But it's obvious."

Henry wouldn't divulge the culprits even if he knew. Too often, the boy genius had found himself upside-down in a garbage can following a smart comment.

"Angled? How's that?"

"Three or four people can pick up a Volkswagen. They picked up one side and rolled it through."

"Not possible," the Director said, measuring the glass sliding doors and his car more closely.

"I can figure it out. Do you have a tape measure?" Henry asked.

Doetkott went off to his apartment and came back to measure the width of his VW at the bumpers and the height at the top of the cab. Henry listened and whipped his slide rule in and out. After running the numbers several ways, he gave up.

"Won't work," he said.

"I told you."

"They removed the fenders," Henry offered.

"None of the bolts have been tampered with. All the street dirt is still there. I checked. And, even with the fenders off, the wheels still won't fit through the door."

Henry manipulated his slide rule again, "However, it might reduce the measurement a few inches."

"Forget it. Nothing has been removed."

After another hour of examining the window and door, Doetkott called maintenance. A few men in blue overalls showed up within minutes.

"They took it apart."

"Nothing has been removed. There is still dirt on all the bolts under the car," he explained.

"They tilted it."

Won't fit that way either," Henry said smugly.

"Even if removed from their frames, the windows are not wide enough," one of the men observed. They too were stumped. The lobby windows were sealed and the sliding doors weren't wide enough, period. They measured several ways, but after another hour, they agreed to call a tow truck.

Throughout the next day, the VW in the lobby received visits from a tow truck operator, the fire department, the police, and a VW auto body guy. None of them could determine how the bug got where it sat. The VW man assured everyone again that no parts had been removed.

"No way it could be tilted," the tow guy assured everyone.

The firemen and police remarked that there were no tire marks on the linoleum floor.

By Wednesday, everyone who lived on campus had come to see the "Bug in the Lobby" caper. Some took photos with their friends sitting on it or pretending to drive. Somebody put a table lamp on the top. Others decorated it with flowers and crepe paper.

Thursday morning, the college newspaper ran a picture of Mac Carpenter, John Alston, Chuck Winters and me standing next to the bug.

At noon, the four of us sat in the dean's office.

"We just saw it there and took a picture with it like everyone else," I explained.

"Right. And, that's why the newspaper picked your photo to run on the front page? I see four very guilty people in this photo," the dean responded. "You have had your fun. Now, get it out of there before the sun goes down, or start packing. Am I clear?"

"Yes sir," we responded as a chorus.

This will take a little explaining. Picture a long, rectangular lounge joining two wings of the dormitory. A wall of sliding glass doors looked out onto lawns to the east and west. At the north end of the lounge, a partitioned TV room sat separated from the main area. It had one exit through two glass doors with panic bars. By removing the center post and the door-returns, we could open the glass doors wide enough to push the VW through with room to spare on each side. But, because the center post appeared permanent, and the doors looked too small even if opened all the way, no one considered this door, even though it was the only other exit. The glass windows and sliding doors were too inviting to the eye. No one could see past the obvious.

As we removed three screws to take out the center pole and door returns, and we opened the doors wide, the Director's wife stood in our path.

"So! This is how you did it."

"We didn't do it. We just figured it out."

She didn't know about the "sweardagod" oath.

"Sure," she said, rolling her eyes.

Before we could push the car into position, she got in it and started the engine right there in the lounge. She made a turn in the lobby, ran it up two steps, hung a left through the two open doors, and drove the car onto the grass toward the street. About half way across the lawn, she came upon the college president and a few visitors who were touring the residence halls together.

"Good morning, Mrs. Doetkott," the president said.

She smiled briefly and continued on her way.

Mr. Doetkott painted over his reserved parking spot. He met with us that night, and we all had a good laugh. He told us about a school on the east coast where some pranksters put a weather balloon in a guy's dorm room and filled it with water during a hard freeze. They left the door and window open, and the water in the balloon froze. Then, they tore the rubber off. When he returned from winter break, he found his room filled with ice.

"What a terrible mess, and an expensive joke," he observed. "Thanks for not damaging my car."

"We just figured it out," I said.

"Yes. That's what my wife said," Doetkott said. "And, I had nothing to do with that balloon thing either."

Later, in my room, John, Mac and Chuck poured ale on my head, chanting, "Long Live the RF King."

Sleeper

In a college dorm, when you play poker with the same guys night after night for months, side bets abound. Anytime a boast takes place, a bet soon follows.

"I can't believe how long I just peed."

"I can go over a minute."

"I went at least two."

"No way."

"I believe it."

"I don't. That's impossible."

"I got a quarter says I can pee *three* minutes," Bill boasted.

"Make it fifty cents and you're on!"

Playing penny-ante, fifty cents represented a whole night's winnings if you got incredibly lucky with cards. We each had to take a portion of this bet as Jackson couldn't front more than a dime.

Mac, the rule maker, said it had to be done within an hour after drinking.

"One time bet. No do-overs. After-squirts don't count. When the steady stream stops, you're done! Got it?"

Bill agreed and prepared himself by chugging as much as he could hold. As we waited for the water to pass through his system, the subject of capacity and penile strength dominated our poker game.

"The smaller the hose, the longer the stream, I say."

"Size had nothing to do with it. It's all about kidneys."

"It's the bladder, not the kidneys."

"I still think the smaller the hose..."

Bill finally said he couldn't hold it any longer.

"This is it, boys. It's *show* time!"

He retired swiftly to the restroom trailed by Mac as his official timer. He denied the rest of us an audience as he said we'd make him nervous. All of us kept very still and listened to the steady stream hitting the toilet bowl as we watched the clock on the wall.

Bill lost.

I don't remember his actual time, but it didn't approach three minutes. He probably could have said two, and we'd have made the same bet.

So it went. We bet on everything.

"I can do fifty sit-ups," Wayne announced on another evening.

"I've done a *hundred*," I said.

"Why don't you stretch a bit?" his roommate Jim asked.

"I can do two hundred," Wayne countered.

"At one time? No rests?"

"I hear a bet," Mac said leaning in from his side of the suite. "Five seconds on his back says he's done."

"How much?"

"I got fifty cents."

On and on. Sit-ups led to chin-ups, push-ups, and the distance one could spit. The same fifty cents moved around us like stocks on Wall Street. Dave tried to set the Guinness World Record of consecutively bouncing a ping-pong ball on a paddle. He fell a few thousand short and had to wear a support on his wrist for weeks.

One night out of nowhere, Bill said, "My roommate could sleep through World War III."

"He's a sleeper, huh?"

"Andy's a sleep machine," Bill said. "And he's got some kind of clock inside him. He goes to bed at different times, doesn't really matter, but when his head hits the pillow he's out cold. At exactly seven every morning, he opens his eyes. No alarm clock. No music. Doesn't matter how much noise I make. Doesn't matter if it's perfectly quiet."

"A sleep machine," I repeated.

Mac considered the possibilities. "Hmm. Your roommate can sleep through anything?"

"Anything," Bill assured us again.

Later that night, Mac led a contingent to Bill's room. We flipped the light switch on and off, talked in normal voices, and banged around a bit. Seeing that we weren't convinced, Bill played a few bars on his trombone. Andy slept like a mummy, wrapped in his bed, not moving a muscle. As we left, we waited and listened at the door just to be sure that we couldn't hear Bill and Andy laughing at our expense.

Back in my room, I suggested we needed to expand our gambling to include others.

"Let's make this one bigger. Let's give outsiders a chance. We can pool our money and make a profit."

"Yeah, let's take the suckers!" Mac added.

"How do we prove we win?" Wayne asked.

"Leave that to me," I said. "I have a great idea."

We emptied our pockets and secret stashes, cashed in all our bottles, and came up with a mutual fund of twenty dollars between the five of us. I waged our bet with several guys based on our having to prove beyond a doubt that Andy could sleep through anything. Within days, everyone in the dorms except Andy had heard about the bet. Our initial twenty dollars soon became a small representation of the volume of side-wagers going down. Odds increased to three-to-one against us. Few people bet in our favor. Everyone assumed that something would wake Andy and we'd lose. We dumped our meager bank accounts, scraped together a second twenty bucks, and bet it all at five-to-one odds. Our funds were exhausted.

191

"We split the initial twenty, plus another hundred with the second twenty, if Andy pulls through," I announced.

"Done deal," Bill assured us.

Wayne had learned about sleep patterns in his psychology class. He told us we needed to wait until Andy had dropped into his deepest slumber.

"Bull," Bill said. "He's gone in thirty seconds."

"Best be safe. It's a lot of money," Mac said. "We'll meet at your room at one o'clock."

When we showed up, Bill had all the lights on and the radio playing.

"I've been trying to stay awake" he said. "I don't know why you needed to wait so long."

Andy slept on his back with the sheet folded tidily over the blanket rimming the bottom of his chin. His head sat perfectly in the middle of the pillow on his twin bed. His mouth drew up in half a smile. Eerie. He looked prepared by a mortician.

"Let's do it," I said.

We needed to prove we won without interference from competitors. The bet said "proof beyond a doubt" so everyone expected us to make the demonstration public. That wouldn't be necessary quite yet.

We tucked Andy's blankets and bedspread firmly into the sides between his mattress and bed frame. Wayne slid under his bed to duck-tape the edges of the blanket securely to the frame. This captured Andy in a blanketed cocoon. Four of us picked him up, bed and all, and slowly turned him to fit out the door. His head fell gently sideways, but the rest of his body remained in position. Once through the door, they righted him, and the rest of his journey was horizontal.

We put the sleeper in my pickup along with half a dozen cinder blocks we borrowed from a construction site. I drove carefully through our quiet town. In my rear-view mirror, I watched the others watching Andy sleep. He looked amazingly peaceful as the street lights flashed across his face. His expression didn't change even though a hank of hair gently flapped in the wind against his forehead. At the center of the small business district, a regal fountain stood in the hub of the Orange City traffic circle. We propped up the four legs of the bed on the four cinder blocks so that Andy could sleep above the two-feet-deep water, a few feet inside the rim of the fountain far enough from the spray not to get him wet. On the remaining two cinder blocks, we placed his bedside table. His clock, wallet, keys, and eyeglasses sat within reach.

In this small college town, passing drivers had grown accustomed to the recurrent suds flowing up over the sides of the central fountain, but they had never seen a man sleeping in a twin bed.

We worried that the noise of the falling water would wake Andy, but it apparently soothed his deepest sleep. We all posed next to the comatose form as Mac took a dozen pictures for the college newspaper. After about an hour, seeing that Andy wasn't going to wake, the guys walked back to the dorms. Bill and I parked the pick-up and caught a nap across the street from the fountain. At six-thirty in the morning, I used a payphone to call Mac. He woke my fellow conspirators, and they alerted everyone who had bet for or against us. Before breakfast and early classes, a parade of college students walked to the town circle to witness the outcome of their wagers.

As the town awoke, the noise of increased commuter traffic filled the circle. Horns honked, drivers whistled, students gathered by the dozens, and a few passers-by stopped to gape and chat. A police patrol car parked behind my truck, and we explained the details of our bet. The cops waited with everyone else to see what would happen.

Andy slept soundly through all the noise.

Sweardagod.

"Simply amazing," said the cop. "This guy is world class."

Promptly at seven, Andy woke, stretched his arms above his head and reached for his glasses. He threw back the bedclothes, swung his feet over the side, and dropped into the fountain. Standing in cold water up to his knees, his bleary eyes focused and his ears tuned in to the sounds coming from a throng of pedestrians cheering, applauding, and howling with laughter on the sidewalk around the fountain.

That evening, in my dorm room, we spread our gambling winnings on my bed and looked at all the money for a while before dividing it between us.

My third consecutive RF award set a record. As far as I know, it still stands.

Doors

In many ways, we were the perfect small college for minority students. Affirmative Action and generous federal grants made college possible. At Chapman in the mid-Sixties, people of color didn't stand out in a crowd. They had numbers. And, we white kids were all the better for the infusion of a new combination of ethnicity and intellect loaded with close family ties, a defined set of cultural mores and spirituality. They brought a refreshing brand of humor, street smarts, card games, pool shooting, and athleticism. Best of all, we white kids were learning to dance ... or, well, sort of.

Compared to the day-to-day trials of growing up in a ghetto, safety to a white kid is usually an illusion. We walk right by danger without ever knowing. In conservative Orange County, despite its surface tranquility, danger lurked just out of sight like a fire-breathing dragon in his cave. I saw this beast come out a couple of times in the Sixties.

The Watts Riots, summer of '66 in nearby Los Angeles, changed everything in the center of conservative Orange County. White people freaked out. Fowler's Gun Shop sold out their entire stock in a few days. The Army-Navy surplus store sold survival gear like never before. People actually boarded up their windows as if a hurricane were on its way.

Driving through Laguna Canyon, returning from a late-night party on the beach, I stopped the car to investigate what looked like a brush fire at the top of a hill. A friend and I hurried up a dirt trail and came within sight of at least a hundred people dressed in white robes and hoods standing in a circle around a tall burning cross. We ran full speed back down the hill.

"Yikes!" my buddy shouted as we leaped back into the car. "Get out of here!"

We weren't in the Deep South. This was Laguna Canyon. But, the mood of paranoia following the riots had swept into the private lives of Orange County. The home county of the John Birch Society obviously welcomed some other extremists as well.

On our campus, our liberal faculty and staff lived in peace with all students, regardless of neighborhood of origin, and they did so by ignoring the signs everywhere around them. Academia has a way of isolating its inhabitants. Most white students were either naïve or ignorant, not having anything to compare to life in the inner cities, and the black and brown kids kept their mouths shut. Most of us thought everybody got along just fine and there didn't need to be a fuss. The fire on the hill frightened me, but soon disappeared in my selective memory.

As a fund-raiser for people who lost property in the Watts Riots, our Black Student Union invited the Harlem Globetrotters to perform at our campus. Tickets sold out in four days. With such a positive response, the Globetrotters offered to play a second game on the following night and give all the proceeds to the charity in addition to the 50% from the first game. Tickets for the second game sold out faster than the first.

The BSU students were elated. This success gave them legitimacy as a campus organization, and it proved that their acceptance as people of color on our campus stood for more than political correctness. They could not have sold that many tickets without the deep support of the white majority.

Unfortunately, somebody forgot to ask permission.

The Dean of Students called an emergency meeting of the Black Student Union and gave them the bad news. The college president had been to an executive meeting of the Board of Trustees where they determined the Harlem Globetrotters were far too volatile for the campus given the racial unrest in nearby L.A. The school didn't have the needed security. The Board had to think about the safety of the students, and the basketball players themselves, and the liabilities were far too great for the campus to risk. The games were off.

"Too soon after the riots. Really sorry, but it's all for the best. Refund the ticket money and do something else."

Never mind that the student organization had signed a binding agreement with the team.

Everyone on campus talked about the Board's decision and little else. We discussed the Globetrotters in the dorms, student union, and cafeteria. A few professors brought it up in class rather than their scheduled lectures. We were living in a fishbowl of political unrest that would not soon be over. Everybody had an opinion.

Together, the campus experienced the first four of the five stages of grief.

Denial: They can't do this. We won't let them. The game will go on. They have no power over us. We control our budget. We can invite whomever we please. We have a contract!

Anger: Who do they think they are? This is blatant racial discrimination, nothing less. This is all the doing of a very conservative Board of Trustees. We'll sue! We'll boycott! At least we'll notify the papers.

Bargaining: What if we take out extra insurance? Can't we beef up campus security with local off-duty policemen? Only Chapman students hold tickets. Nothing's been advertised. Who are we afraid of? Most local off-campus citizens won't even know.

Regardless of our attempts to negotiate, the gap widened between the decision-makers and the messengers. Our own dean and president tried to represent us, but they only got a more firmly negative response from the Board. The pronouncement was final. No further discussion. *Depression* hit the entire campus. For two weeks, people abandoned public areas. Activities ceased. The athletic field stood inactive. No one felt like having a good time. Some faculty members canceled classes. The library looked like a tomb. Perpetual bridge games in the student union folded for the first time in decades. The snack bar was empty. The jukebox sat strangely mute, its fluorescent lights buzzing and flickering in the dark. Students came to the cafeteria, ate their food, and left with little conversation. The reality of our powerlessness buried us. No one wanted to discuss it. We had no recourse. Our administrators were dismayed but helpless. The Board of Trustees, absent and non-approachable, had brought down an ax on the campus that they could not feel or understand. A few frightened men had made a safe decision at a protected distance, hiding behind their authority and anonymity.

They thought they were doing the right thing, the mature thing. We thought they were cowards.

The fifth stage, *Acceptance*, didn't come. We languished in depression. Although the Board assumed the campus mood would pass, it lingered and festered. Professors met their classes in off-campus coffee houses and their own homes. From behind closed office doors, one could hear whispers at private special meetings. The student newspaper ran a special one-page issue that said only "shame" in bold letters across the front and chronicled the Board's decision on the back. The Music Department cancelled an orchestra concert as no one picked up their free tickets, and most of the musicians called in sick. Worst of all, black and white students uncommonly segregated. No matter what we did, no matter how we felt or what we said to each other, we just weren't comfortable in our own skins – black or white.

198

The president of the student body called a meeting in the auditorium. Almost everybody showed up. The Black Student Union members occupied the front row.

"This is a rare and special time. Nobody can remember the faculty ever agreeing on anything, but they are obviously 100% on our side," he stated, and asked us to go back to classes, not to hurt our own education, not to take out our disappointment on our professors who, although they were seemingly helpless, were nevertheless in the students' corner. He said he and our other student representatives had worked very hard, night and day, but had come up with nothing but failure. To paraphrase the final words of his speech, "We have tried to open the door of communications with the Administration, but they have refused. To be fair, our college president and his staff are in a tight situation. They cannot, they dare not, refute the orders of our benefactors. The Trustees are responsible for the financial and physical security of our college, and they have acted with that in mind. Although I do not support their decision, and I know that the majority of the people in this room agree with me, that door has closed. There is nothing we can do but accept it and move on."

He had entered his *acceptance* stage.

"The door is closed," I said to my gang of buddies. "He has given up. Now we have no representation. We have no voice."

"So how do we get the doors open?" Mac asked.

"We protest. We stage a riot!" Jackson suggested. "I'm so mad, I could...."

"Whoa, big fella," Mac interrupted. "That's going to bring the hammer down harder."

"We need to negotiate," I suggested. "We need a bargaining chip."

"Pre-registration is coming up," Wayne noted. "We could have a shut-down. We could get the majority not to register for next semester. That would get the Board's attention."

"Good thinking," Mac said. "But, impossible. Support will diminish between now and pre-registration. It's already been over a week and people are giving up already."

"Plus that just hurts us getting the classes we need," Chuck added.

"We need to do something now," I said. "Today."

"But, what?" they all asked.

"The doors are closed," I repeated, thinking aloud. "The doors are closed."

My creativity has always been enhanced when under pressure and in front of an audience. My buddies watched me pace back and forth. I could feel that old charge coming.

"The administration building has doors with hinges on the outside. We need to open the doors," I said with a sly smile.

"Open the doors?" Mac asked.

"Let's go over there and check it out right now," I said.

"I'm in!"

"Me too!"

"Wait. What?" Wayne asked.

We ran to the campus, Wayne trying to keep up and asking questions as we trotted.

"See, as I told you," I said, pointing to the entrance doors.

"So are these," Mac said, sticking his head back out the door.

We ran inside and right up to the Business Office. Outside hinges! Directly across the hall, the president's office door had the same hinges. Chuck, Mac and Jackson went to the other end of the lobby.

"So are these," they yelled.

We scampered around the three floors of the Ad Building and found every hall door vulnerable.

"Somebody wasn't thinking."

"This building is about a hundred years old. They used to build them this way when security wasn't an issue," Mac observed. "They hung all the doors so they would open into the hallway. It was probably a fire law."

"Whatever the reason," I said. "We only need a small hammer and a screwdriver."

At one o'clock in the morning after our lone night security officer had gone home, I entered the Administration Building through a window we had left open in a daylight basement bathroom. Through a side door, I let in twenty of our friends. In less than two hours, we had removed the brass cylinders holding the hinges on every door in the entire building. We even took the doors off the stalls in the restrooms.

We picked a spot to hide the doors out of view of any curious maintenance worker. My crew carried the heavy doors across the quad and carefully slipped them through a window we pried open in the unused crawl space of an adjacent building. They were carefully stacked and covered with tarps. Our booty lay safely hidden about a hundred feet from where they came. I closed the window and nailed it shut again from the inside.

The following morning, the president found a note on his desk.

We'd like to "open the doors" to the Board
of Trustees concerning the Globetrotters."

For two days Maintenance and Security looked for the doors. On the third day, they called in the local police. No one could find the doors.

"Those things are heavy," the maintenance director said. "They can't have taken them far. Not without a huge truck."

Aggravation overcame the administration. The dean threatened expulsion of the Black Student Union leaders. They insisted they knew nothing. During the week following, every student leader on campus found himself or herself in the dean's office being threatened with severe discipline, even expulsion, if they didn't come up with the perpetrators.

Nobody knew anything.

"This is impossible!" cried the dean. "Something like this does not happen in a vacuum!"

Finally, somebody spoke up and suggested that anything as inventive and effective as the door caper had to be the work of the reigning RF King. Later that day, I received a polite phone call from the president's secretary inviting me to "drop by for a visit with Dr. Davis."

"We know you are involved," the dean said.

"I noticed the doors were missing," I said.

"Either tell us where they are, or you are history!"

"Is this why you asked me here?" I said directly to President Davis.

"You will only get yourself further in trouble by lying, young man," the dean warned, interrupting the president who had taken a breath to speak.

"Why were they taken?" I asked.

"We don't *know* why. Don't play with me!"

"Now who is lying?" I asked the dean.

I looked back at the Dr. Davis who everyone knew to be a very fair man.

"It's about this Globetrotter thing," he said barely audibly. "That's all we know. They left a note."

"Which is none of your concern," the dean added, now beginning to redden around the collar.

I continued to play dumb. "Everyone knows it's about the Globetrotters. That decision killed the spirit of this campus. But why the doors?"

"You are excused, young man!" the dean exploded. "If you refuse to be honest with us, we will be dealt with harshly

I called my dad, an graduate of Chapman who had earned the Alumnus of the Year Award ten years earlier. I told him why I might be coming home unexpectedly. I explained to him the facts of the scandal as best I could. I admitted moving the doors and asked his advice.

My father took the news unexpectedly calmly. If anyone loved basketball, and especially the Harlem Globetrotters, my dad did. He had lettered all four years in basketball at Chapman. He called one of his oldest friends, who also happened to be the son of the founder of the college, Ernie Chapman. The next morning, I received a call to return to the president's office.

"I talked to your father this morning, Ben," President Davis said. "He is concerned that you might be coming home early this semester."

"Yes," I said. "I hear a lot of people might be doing that."

"Well, we're not going to let that happen. Let's all be grown up about this. We can't have students disappearing, and I can't really conduct business without any doors in the building now, can I?"

"No sir."

The dean interrupted. "OK, Ben. You played your ace. Now, what do you want?"

"I can't say where your doors are. But, I can tell you how to get them back."

"Go ahead. We're listening."

"Open the dialogue with the BSU to come up with a fair way that allows the games to be played. Make it safe for the Globetrotters and the students, and risk-free for the college."

"The Board of Trustees will not allow it."

"Racial prejudice," I said. "This is nothing more than bigotry!"

"Nobody said anything about race," the dean interjected. "That is insubordination!"

No one spoke as the dean's voice continued to echo, as did my blatant accusation. A gloom hung in the office. I had uttered the unmentionable. None of us came to this table with a political agenda. We were each responsible to our constituents according to our loyalties, and by our values. When I realized that the other two were as trapped as I, an unusual sense of peace came from somewhere. The darkness lifted. I became aware of the sunlight glowing in a tree outside the president's window. I felt a force that might allow us to trust each other. I took a breath to say where the doors were hidden.

I didn't get the chance.

"That is *exactly* what this is about," the president blurted. "It's the thing nobody wants to talk about!"

His eyes became soft and he smiled at me then spoke to the dean. "When we have lost our way, our children will lead us."

"Your hands are tied here," the dean said. "All our hands are tied."

"Perhaps you're right. But, I think it is time I showed a little leadership," the president said, right there in front of the dean and me. Sweardagod.

I wish I had been there to hear Dr. Davis address the executive committee of the Board. Their meeting lasted most of the next morning in a conference room behind the open gaps that used to be heavy wooden doors. Security officers in the hallway kept people from walking too close. Speeches were made, all of the board members were consulted by phone, and new decisions were ultimately made. The president submitted his resignation early in the meeting, but it wasn't accepted. With the insistence of the board secretary, the founder's son who had remained silent until that point, the full board agreed to allow Dr. Davis to run his campus as he saw fit.

The dean called a meeting of the student council and the BSU. They told him that the Globetrotters had booked themselves into another college to cover both dates. Tickets had been refunded. They made plans to bring the famous basketball team back the following semester.

I stopped by to see the head of maintenance and told him where the doors were located. I offered student assistance in helping to carry the heavy doors and re-hang them where they belonged. He declined. When his men crawled under the building and made their way to the back, under several weathered tarps they found neatly stacked oak doors with notes on each indicating their original location. The next morning, administrators came to work and unlocked their office doors to begin a more normal day.

Several weeks later, the president of the Black Student Union came to my room and asked me how many people it took to remove and carry the doors.

"About twenty of us," I said.

He gave me a voucher for twenty tickets to one of the Globetrotters games the next semester and asked me to be his campaign manager when he ran for president of the student body. I agreed, and we won by a landslide.

Triplets

The first triplets I ever knew were Jim, Joan and John Spitler. The two boys came to Chapman the year after I did. Their sister, Joan, remained at home in Stockton where she attended the College of the Pacific. They explained that they would have all come but that having all three leave home would have been too traumatic for their mom.

John and Jim were not roommates. They didn't dress alike or take the same classes. Although they looked exactly like each other, they were of course fraternal triplets, being that one of the three came out female. A picture of Joan sat on each of their dorm desks and was, everyone agreed, drop-dead gorgeous. Her long, straight black hair and big blue eyes defied resistance. Friends of the boys often tried to get them to coax their sister down for a visit, and possibly a date. The waiting list grew every time somebody got a glance.

Joan often came up in our discussions. Every guy knew what bragging rights would come from any kind of nod from the queen of everyone's fantasies, the gal distant enough to cause no threat, to never say no, the one who sat silently behind glass and smiled eternally from her frame of exclusion. Although none of us had ever met her, something about a picture on a guy's desk had an allure. Her distance and the protection of two strong brothers gave her mystical magnetism.

207

"I hear Joan's coming to Homecoming," Bill announced one night. "She's supposedly agreed to go to the dance with someone, but nobody knows who."

"So who do we know who doesn't have a date yet," I asked.

"Everybody," Mac said.

We all laughed. None of us yet had a date for the homecoming dance.

"Well, it's not me," Bill said. "I'm going with Linda."

"You are?"

"I am. She doesn't know that yet. But we're going. It's a sure thing," Bill insisted.

So it went, through the next four weeks. One at time, each of us found a date and eliminated ourselves from the Joan homecoming mystery.

"We should start a pool," the chronic gambler Mac suggested with just over two weeks to go. "We know that none of us are going with Joan because we all have dates now. But we should put all the other potential guys in a hat and draw names."

"How much?" I asked.

"A buck per name," Mac said.

We each drew two names out of the hat and put in a dollar for each. The kitty held ten dollars. I drew Frank, Johns' roommate, and a long-shot named Matt who barely knew Jim and John. Moderately handsome, pockets full of daddy's money, he had a car.

"I'm looking very good," I said, trying to show confidence.

"Side bet Ben wins with the dark horse Matt." Wayne offered.

"Ugh, Matt the Mod?"

"Mr. Tall, Dark and Hands?"

"He's got a car and women dig him," Wayne said. "I wish I had half his throwaways."

"Count Matt out," Mac said. "He's in there because he's eligible, but I don't see John and Jim allowing him within a mile of their sister.

Homecoming came after a week of speculations and more side bets. I lost Frank when he announced that he would be escorting Tina, one of the Homecoming Queen candidates. Matt became my only chance. I knew better than to count on the ten dollars.

News of other dates found more candidates falling by the side of the road. With two days to go, the front-runner was Mac's pick, Charlie, Jim's roommate.

"Side bet on it being no one we picked," somebody offered.

Nobody bit. Our life savings were all in the hat.

John, Jim and Charlie said nothing. My pick, Matt, remained oblivious. When asked about homecoming, he feigned no interest.

"Right," Mac observed. "He says he's not going. How do we know?"

"Mac's got it with Charlie," I told Jackson. "Wayne saw him at the florist ordering a corsage."

"No way! Are we supposed to be getting flowers for Homecoming?" Jackson asked.

"I thought only the guys escorting the queen candidates bought flowers," Bob added.

"You're right. I'm not buying flowers," Jackson assured us.

"But, for Joan Spitler?" Mac observed. We all nodded in agreement.

When Homecoming arrived, the student body president crowned the queen at a morning ceremony. We ate lunch in the well-decorated cafeteria. The queen and her court drifted in wearing their formals with a hundred slips hidden beneath their long gowns.

While we prepared to go to the game, Jim and John borrowed a car to pick up their sister at the Orange County

Airport. We were all waiting in the parking lot, but they snuck her in the back way just to add to the suspense. Right up to the final hour, none of us knew who would be escorting our fantasy girl to the game and the dance.

Matt didn't come through for me. He left campus for the weekend.

Seconds before the tip-off to our homecoming basketball game, planned for exactly when everyone would be in the stands and they would enjoy their best audience, Jim's roommate Charlie walked in with Miss America herself on his arm. She looked more beautiful in person than any of us expected. Her short skirt revealed long chiseled legs that ran four blocks down to stiletto high heels. Her slender figure seemed to sway like a palm tree in a tropical breeze.

For a moment, oxygen became scarce as everyone in the gymnasium simultaneously drew in their breath.

"Mac wins," I whispered.

"Charlie wins," Mac said, correcting me. "Just *look* at her."

"Oh my!" Bob muttered. "She's even cuter than her picture."

"I'm losing consciousness," Jackson added. "I need air."

"I need *her*," Bob said.

"You need a grasp on reality," Mac said.

Somebody in the back of the stands gave out a loud whistle, and the entire gymnasium broke into laughter. Obviously, everyone had stopped to look at the same thing.

Charlie and Joan found a seat at the end of the bleachers and for the next forty-five minutes our eyes couldn't decide between her and the game. At half time, it looked like a wedding reception as guys and gals crowded around the stranger from the north. Jim stood nearby, proud and smiling like the father of the bride. Charlie didn't really know what to do with himself. He stood with his hands thrust into his pockets and his shoulders hunched forward, looking down at the floor. Nobody gave him much notice. Joan absorbed everything, obviously familiar with being the center of attention. There were even a couple of flashes from someone's camera which she responded to like a starlet, showing her bright eyes and straight teeth in a rehearsed pose.

Charlie lost out. Other guys stepped forward to make their best pitches to Joan. I felt sorry for the Homecoming Queen and her court standing at the other side of the gym lobby, neglected in their formals and flowers, waiting for someone to gush over them. No one could deny the radiance of the uncrowned princess. One quick smile and you were absorbed.

At the dance, she continued her reign. Every guy waited for his turn to share center stage with the precocious and flirtatious Joan Spitler. Charlie almost disappeared. Either Jim or John would show up periodically to save Joan when her suitors became too obvious or grabby. Her brothers seemed to know just when to courteously slip her away to grab a glass of punch or escape outside for fresh air. They had been through this before. Joan giggled and excused herself, promising the next dance. Charlie spent most of the evening sulking at a table alone, feeling way out of his league. This beauty queen of flirtatious small talk, belle of the ball, walking dream, brought too many levels of sophistication for him to handle.

Too soon, it all came to an end. As a group of friends, we walked slowly with our dates two blocks back to the dormitories to have all the girls in by midnight. Charlie had disappeared. Jim went off somewhere, probably making out with his date in his borrowed car. Therefore, Joan walked back with her brother John, his date, and several other couples. When we got to the dorms, John said goodnight, and Joan accompanied him up three flights of external stairs to his dorm room.

"No way," Wayne whispered. "She can't go up there! Doesn't matter if she's his sister."

Girls were absolutely forbidden from the boy's dorms. This non-negotiable law eased only on the first and last days of school. Any other time, not even mothers were allowed. If caught, it meant being kicked out of the dorms. Since freshmen were required to live on campus, for John it meant expulsion.

We all watched them ascend the steps to his room on the third floor. We hollered for them to come back.

"John, no!"

"You'll get caught!"

Jim and John had never done anything wrong or even out of the ordinary. They were model students, both making straight-As, and each had applied for Resident Advisor for their sophomore year. Until this miscalculation, John had been a natural selection. Nevertheless, there he went, walking up the external stairwell to the second floor with his sister.

"She's not going to sleep in his room, is she?" Jackson asked.

"This is bad news," Mac said. "The RD will find out. Somebody is bound to talk."

We looked around and there were indeed a bunch of guys watching the two ascend the stairs.

"Hey, John. Come on. Don't!" Jackson shouted.

"Come back down!"

"John, please!"

The pair ignored us as they passed the landing between the second and third floors. Joan seemed to be giving us the benefit of swinging her hips a bit more aggressively.

"Nothing's going to happen up there with her brother," I suggested.

"Doesn't matter," Mac reminded me. "The chick rule has no exceptions, period!"

We watched with our mouths wide open. One of the nicest guys in the residence halls was about to go down in flames. Not two seconds after the door closed to John's dorm room on the third floor, the Resident Director's door burst open. He stormed past all of us straight to the steps.

Our stomachs dropped as he reached the second landing.

"Somebody call John," Jackson said.

"It's too late," Mac observed. "Where will she go now?"

"She could escape through the bathroom and run out their suitemate's door."

"Too late, he's there."

We watched as the RD arrived at John's dorm room and banged loudly.

"John. Open the door *now*. I know you're in there!"

Out of breath and impatient, when the door did not open readily, he reached for his passkey and stuck it in the lock.

"I'm going to use my key, John. Open up!"

Turning the key and pushing the door open, he came back out from the room so fast that he almost launched himself backwards over the third floor railing. Laughter exploded from inside the room.

We all hustled up the steps taking three at a time. Arriving at John's room, our RD stood there with his hand against his chest, breathing hard, pointing at the door.

"Go ahead," he gasped.

When Mac pushed the door wide, we all saw Joan sitting spread-eagle at the foot of the bed. She lifted her short skirt exposing us to the fact that "she" was, in fact, "he." We too leaped back in horror.

Jim Spitler had pulled off the most remarkable gender change I have ever seen.

During the game and dance, John had changed his coat and tie repeatedly to appear on and off as first himself and then his brother. None of us noticed that the two boys never appeared at the same time. Jim seemed to be having so much fun with his date, we all assumed they kept disappearing to make out.

When the Resident Director regained his senses, he asked the boys how they'd done it.

"Spent the entire day in make-up," Jim explained. "First, I had to shave closely. Then, Robyn plucked my brows, shaved my sideburns, smeared heavy pancake on my whole face, and applied junk to my eyes and cheeks and lips. She did a pretty good job. After a couple of hours, when I looked in the mirror, I couldn't believe who I saw."

"The hair is the best," I observed. "That's what got me."

"Robyn again. This is real hair. It's a very expensive wig. It belongs to Robyn's mom."

"How long have you been planning this?"

"With Robyn? About two weeks. We let her in because we needed clothes. Robyn and I are about the same size. This is all her stuff except the shoes. I bought the shoes for a quarter at Goodwill. Big mistake. They nearly killed me."

"I mean, how long have you and John been planning this?" Mac asked.

Jim removed his wig. More of the male appeared. His hairy chest was revealed under the stuffed bra. He wiped the lipstick from his face as his brother explained.

"Last year, we came here on Senior Visit Day. That morning, a student woke up sleeping in the fountain down at the circle. Our tour guide told us about the notorious RF King."

"We were big on pranks in high school. All the way home to Stockton, we talked about RFs," John continued. "Last year, Jim and I sang a girl-boy duet for Senior Skits. Right then we decided that we'd include Joan in our plans for college. We took pictures and began plotting."

214

That night, the triplets who were really twins were crowned RF Kings. The each got crowns, a beer anointing, and chanting from their peers. I lost my title and never tried to gain it back.

Music

My dad played clarinet, and we grew up listening to swing band and Dixieland jazz records. My first sentence may have been, "Daddy, toot your horn." Church added old gospel influence. My first AM radio, which I tuned to a Saturday morning kiddy show called Big John and Sparky, featured only two kinds of music: country and western. I often went to sleep to the Grand Old Opry, becoming a fan of Patsy Cline, Hank Williams, Loretta Lynn and Bob Wills. Then, in 1956, "Rock Around the Clock" by Bill Haley and the Comets, initiated a genre that would drastically change and never leave the landscape. Others have tried to renew, remake or re-invent rock and roll, but the Oldies stations still outplay all the others combined.

In the turmoil of the Seventies when a lot of popular music turned very dark, atonal, lewd, and loud, I escaped to folk rock. Living in Texas in the Eighties, I naturally listened to vintage country having memorized all the lyrics when I was younger. Then, moving to the northwest in the Nineties, I returned to oldies, jazz and classical.

I can still sink or rise to any mood by flipping on the correct music. I can stroll down memory lane, remembering exactly where I was when I heard a particular song.

Working first in the Entertainment Division at Disneyland, followed by fifteen years as a student activities director for two small universities, I have worked with many talented musicians. After concerts, they often stayed at my house, and we played music into the wee hours of the morning. Some of them became successful, but most lived only to play their music, campus to campus, town to town, making barely enough to pay gas to the next gig. It didn't really matter to me. The short time I had with each of them was golden.

My daughters were introduced to music via the jukebox in the playroom. I could control their tastes with the 45s I chose to put in the box. Their friends are still amazed at how they know the lyrics to so many old tunes. I raised them on songs so we could sing and dance together, and I told them stories about wonderful musicians.

Sailor

On Christmas Eve, there was no parade scheduled. Arrangements with others for dinner fell through as they each begged off to join their families at home. Being 400 miles from my own family and living alone, I decided Disneyland would be just as good as any place to spend the holiday evening.

After a nice dinner at the employee cafeteria, I wandered into the Park. On a corner of Town Square, the Wurlitzer Shop displayed a dozen beautiful pianos from vintage to the latest models. A crowd had formed around a sailor in full dress whites sitting at a baby grand piano playing Christmas Carols. People quietly hummed along when someone started singing the words out loud. Everyone automatically broke into full choruses of the familiar tunes.

We echoed four-part harmonies for at least an hour, laughing with each other after each song as if we were breaking some kind of rule about singing in public. While the young man concentrated on the keys in front of him, playing every song from memory, someone stepped forward and discretely removed the sailor's white cap from the piano bench. At first, I wondered what he was doing. Then, I saw him put a bill in the hat and pass it to the person next to him.

As the sailor accepted his final ovation and stood to leave, he turned to retrieve his cap. He found it filled to the brim with fives, tens and twenties. He sat back down on the bench and peered at the cash through stinging eyes.

Christmas Eve and away from home, he couldn't hold back. Tears rolled down his cheeks. Everyone soon joined him. Grown men. Little kids. All total strangers. We grinned uncontrollably and let our tears flood our faces. Kleenex passed freely from hand to hand.

It felt like we had all accidentally fallen into the way things are supposed to be ... always. Say what you want about Disney magic, it was my best Christmas ever.

Modulation

Each summer, Country Sundays brought some of the finest people in the music "bidness" to Disneyland. I stage-managed shows for down-home folks like Roy Clark, Loretta Lynn, Mel Tillis, Doug Kershaw, and Buck Owens, all of them kind, polite, gentle, and charming.

When the headliner didn't bring a band, Disneyland supplied top-notch studio musicians to provide backup. In summer of 1968, Tony Booth and his band were our host musicians. Archie played drums and didn't say much. The leader, Tony, played acoustic guitar and supplied background vocals. His brother Larry played bass and sang. The lead guitarist, Al Bruno, and the steel player, J.D. Manus, were both well-known throughout the industry. Their names appear on the backs of many record albums.

We worked together every Sunday for twelve weeks from June to September. Our schedule included a rehearsal in the afternoon where I got to watch how professionally the house band read new charts and assimilated all the necessary keys, leads, changes, and breaks. Guest performers always complimented the boys on their skills. Rehearsals went without even the slightest problem.

All except one.

Older male stars often travel with a young up-and-comer female performer who would perform a song or two during the show. Many of the big names carried at least one unknown with their entourage. One memorable singer seemed younger and less road-worthy than most.

Al Bruno led the rehearsal. The gal had only one song. The band played, and she sang it once perfectly. At the end, Al asked her if she was happy.

"Yes. You guys are really good," she said.

"So, this is pretty straight forward. Is everybody okay?" Al asked the other band members. Everyone nodded.

"We caught the modulation coming out of the bridge," J.D. observed.

"Yes, we all got that," Al agreed.

"What modulation?" the singer asked.

Huh?

Oops.

The band members looked at each other, and every eye eventually focused on Al Bruno.

"After the bridge," he said to the gal. "We modulated from D major to E major. Was that a mistake?"

"There is no modulation," she insisted.

"Okay. No sweat. Can we take it again?"

"Sure," she said, looking inquisitively.

"Al?" Tony asked.

Bruno gave the band a downbeat and played his part leading into the bridge. The boys caught on by the third beat. The young singer held the microphone to her mouth and picked right up where Al started. When she ended the bridge and started into the final chorus, she clearly modulated from D to E.

Al waved to stop the band.

"Right there," he said. "We were here..." he played a few chords in D, "... and we went here," he slid up a step to E. "That is where we modulated."

"That isn't a modulation," she said. "It was written that way!"

The band stood like statues for several seconds. I stepped forward from the side of the stage.

"Well, boys, can you play it exactly like it was written?" I asked.

"Right," Al said.

"Yes. Thanks," Tony echoed.

Fifteen minutes later, and not until the dressing room door was shut tightly behind us, we all broke up. After that day, every time a modulation occurred in anybody's music, Al, Archie, Tony, Larry, and J.D. looked over to my side of the stage and mouthed the words, "It was written that way."

Harmonicas

The National Association for Campus Activities is the organization that grew out of the old College Circuit which started when entertainers would agree to play at several campuses within close proximity for a lower price if they would agree on a string of dates. Called Co-Op Booking, this has helped launch many young careers.

As a lover of acoustic guitar music, I would make any excuse to gather players around me. In the evenings at conferences, I hosted picker parties in my hotel suite in which the entertainers would share a new tune they were working on, or something everyone knew well enough that we could sing along. At one such party, the subject of harmonicas came up. A group called The Shoppe had showcased at the convention, and they were sitting in my room late at night. One of the guests asked them how they got together. The story ended with the acquisition of their latest performer, an excellent mouth harp player.

"We found him at a college playing in a small country band," the leader explained. "Since we had lost our fiddle player, we agreed that his harmonica could fill that hole."

"He negotiated hard," joked another member of The Shoppe.

"No I didn't," the harmonica player said. "I came way too easy."

"We asked what it would take for him to leave college and come on the road with us," the leader explained. "He said... well, you tell them."

The harp player continued, "I had seen the Dillards in concert. Rodney Dillard brought out a little case with a dozen harmonicas. I thought that I would do anything to have a set like that."

"Done deal," The Shoppe leader said. "We bought him brand new harmonicas in every key."

"And this beautiful carrying case."

He opened the box, pulled out a harmonica, and played a familiar melody. Several guitarists picked up the key and began to strum along.

"Hey wait," said a guest standing against the wall. The music stopped. He was a tall athletic-looking student. "Why don't you pass out the rest of those harmonicas so we *all* can play?"

Five

Three chords are all you need to sing a hundred folk songs. I first learned to play a ukulele. Most people don't know it, but a ukulele is tuned the same as the highest four strings of a guitar. When we formed a small band, my buddy Dean found me a four-string tenor guitar. It made me look more legitimate and less like I was strumming for a luau.

Nick Reynolds of the Kingston Trio played a tenor guitar. Unknown to me, it required different tuning and very complicated fingering, but I just tuned mine like a uke and twanged my heart out. I watched Dean's fingers on his guitar and copied what he played on his first four strings. I never got very good, but I could match the chords.

Years later, working for the Entertainment Division at Disneyland, I managed shows on various Disneyland stages. My frustration as a musician after one mundane year in a nowhere group gave me a fond appreciation for professional musicians. I eagerly accepted every assignment to work with live shows.

At the end of each school year, Disneyland hosted grad parties for high school seniors. Twenty or thirty schools shared the park with free access to all the attractions. I loved working late in the evening till sunrise. I worked with many future and past entertainers.

I sat with two up-and-coming stars, Glenn Campbell and Kenny Rogers, at Howard Johnson's one morning following a long night of performing for less than appreciative high school kids. The two pickers discussed

227

their country music careers and, with apologies to me, agreed that Disneyland Grad Parties had to be the lowest they had fallen.

Listening to them, I learned that Glen Campbell had previously played guitar for Elvis, Frank Sinatra, Dean Martin, Frankie Avalon, The Mamas and Papas, The Association, and even for the Monkees on "I'm a Believer," one of my all-time favorite songs. He had even briefly replaced Brian Wilson as one of the Beach Boys. Wow!

Kenny Rogers had started with the New Christie Minstrels but they had flamed out soon after lit. He founded the First Edition with some of his friends from the Minstrels, but they were constantly frustrated with record labels and producers ignoring what they knew were potential hits.

Breakfast ended with talks of thoroughbreds and how raising and trading horses had to be more lucrative than playing at the Magic Kingdom. Glenn and Kenny promised each other that they would move together to Montana and raise thoroughbreds if something didn't happen soon. In a few months, Glen Campbell's release of "By the Time I Get to Phoenix" hit number two on the pop charts. Shortly thereafter, Kenny Rogers and the First Edition made an equal splash with "Just Dropped In" and "Ruby, Don't Take Your Love to Town."

The horses would have to wait.

Grad party acts were what we called "one hit wonders." One such group had produced only one recognizable song, "You Were on My Mind," a nonsensical jingle with repetitive lyrics. It had nevertheless put We Five in the music business. They opened and closed every set with their only familiar tune.

When I woke up this morning, you were on my mind
And you were on my mind
I got troubles, whoa-oh, I got worries, whoa-oh,
I got wounds to bind.

So I went to the corner, just to ease my pain,
Yeah, just to ease my pain.
I got troubles, etc.
When I woke up this morning, etc.

Mike Stewart, Beverly Bivens, and Jerry Burgan were the nucleus of We Five. They showed up for their all-nighter with two sidemen who weren't from the original band. The eighteen-year-olds wouldn't notice.

I made polite conversation with Jerry between sets.

"Can you help me understand those lyrics?" I asked.

"You mean the deep, sensitive, socially-redeeming poetry hidden within the fabric of a blissful melody?" he asked.

"Yeah. Whatever."

"They mean absolutely nothing."

"Huh?"

"They were written very late one night. They are nonsense. I'm so tired of that song, I could throw up."

"Where did you come up with a name like We Five?" I asked.

"That's an old story," he said. "Mike Stewart and I played together in high school, inspired by his brother, John."

"John Stewart. Yes. I'm a big fan of the Kingston Trio," I responded. "I played tenor guitar like Nick Reynolds."

"You wanna sit in for our next set?"

"You really don't want that," I said. "I'm much better backstage."

He cocked one eyebrow and continued his story.

"We had several chick singers over the years, and each of them came and went with awful names for our group. When we heard Bev sing, we knew she would stay but, unlike her predecessors, she had no brilliant ideas for a band name. We met our guitar player, Bob Jones, at University of

229

San Francisco in '63. He too had lousy ideas for names. Remember Moby Grape and Iron Butterfly?"

"I remember. How about Credence Clearwater Revival?"

"We had a softer sound. We needed a folksy name. But, if we followed Peter, Paul and Marry, we'd be Mike, Jerry, Bev, Pete and Bob."

"Not exactly catchy," I laughed.

"And combinations of our last names like the Everly Brothers or Simon & Garfunkle were even worse. Meanwhile, even though our recording of *You Were on My Mind* wasn't one of our best, it hit the charts."

"But it had 'We Five' on it, I know. I bought a copy." I said.

"Good for you. When we heard from the studio that they wanted to release it for general radio play as a single, we needed to come up with a name. We only had a week! Mike's brother, John, had invited us to a hootenanny where the Kingston Trio was headlining. We drove up from the Bay Area to Sacramento because it might be televised locally and the exposure couldn't hurt. Tired from playing late the night before, and irritated to be up so early on the road, we bickered about our name for miles. Bev begged us to stop. She said she'd scream if she heard one more suggestion about a name. 'Wait for a sign,' she said. 'Something will come up if you just have faith.' I spent the rest of the trip scanning the passing billboards for an inspiration."

He described waiting to go on still waiting for inspiration. "In about two minutes, we were going onstage as 'The Stupid Band with No Ideas.' Meanwhile, the little group singing before us caught my attention. They were four inexperienced high school kids. The two guitars strummed the same chords, and the bass player fumbled for his notes. The chick singer sounded so nervous, I thought she might wet her pants. Her voice cracked, and she forgot some of the lyrics. I told Mike that I didn't mind following this bunch. He agreed that they were terrible. This would hopefully be their last performance. The announcer gave them the benefit of doubt as he shouted 'We Four' into the microphone. 'The We Four!' Nobody applauded, not even politely."

Jerry sighed, "They were just awful. As I watched those four kids walk off the stage into oblivion, hanging their heads, I felt bad for them. As we took the stage, the MC asked me for our name. 'We *FIVE!*' I said, making fun of his attempt to hype that awful quartet. He laughed at my sarcasm and announced us using that name. 'Going them one better,' he shouted into his microphone, 'Now, ladies and gentlemen, please welcome the *We Five!*' It stuck. That is exactly how we got our name. We stole it from those poor kids before us."

"I grew up in Sacramento," I told Jerry, "and, I never missed a hootenanny. That was at the El Rancho Hotel in 1963. I got a Kingston Trio album autographed by Nick Reynolds."

"You were there? No kidding? Wow! Did you hear us play?" Jerry asked.

"No. We were commiserating in the hotel lobby. See, I was the tenor guitar player in The Whee Four."

Jerry dropped his jaw and gaped at me.

"Sweardagod," I said, crossing my heart.

"Holy crap!" Jerry exploded. "Bev, Michael, come *here!* You are not going to *believe* who I'm talking to."

He looked at me apologetically, "Oh my god, I am so sorry."

"It's okay," I said. "We really stunk."

Synchronicity

"The farther I wake into this life, the more I realize that God is everywhere and the extraordinary lies quietly waiting beneath the skin of all that is ordinary."

Mark Nepo

I believe synchronicities are a salutation, like a cosmic attention-getter. "Hey! How ya doin'? Are ya payin' attention?" Yes, I believe they come directly from the Spirit. There are just too many of them for me to make other rationalizations. I think one of the hardest things for mortals to accept is that we're not alone, and that we don't need to fear the unknown. We spend a lot of energy and get all balled up trying to define the Creator so we can assume dominion. It would be better to accept that we're subjects and stewards of an indefinable creation, that we're all connected to each other, and that the Spirit would like to be included in that relationship.

I don't find deep meaning in every synchronicity. Some of them just remind me that the Creator has a sense of humor. Nevertheless, I am here for a purpose whether I acknowledge it or not. In my constant push and pull to maintain control, as arrogant as that is, I often need a gentle tap to reconnect me with what is generative and sustaining, what is principled and right, what is clear and visionary.

Sometimes, it's harder than a tap.

Brother

Vincent and I shared the graveyard shift at Tripler Army Medical Center in Honolulu. We were in Vietnam together and came back from the jungle war to a beautiful paradise. When given the choice of where we'd like to work, we asked for the same duty station.

We both grew up with sisters. Our comfort with each other was like finding a long-lost brother. We shared so many things in common that we jokingly referred to each other as "twin."

We spent every waking hour together discussing life, plotting our next moves, imagining the future, and talking about what we were going to do when we got out of the army. Every day brought another brilliant scheme of how we might travel, or find the perfect women, or buy our favorite car, or start a band. We had dozens of ideas about launching a business together.

Vincent and I were going through emotional rehabilitation without the assistance of a therapist. As medics in Vietnam, we had been through an experience that we couldn't talk about yet, but we could rediscover normal life in the safety and beauty of Hawaii as we loosened the grip of our battlefield memories.

Vincent routinely introduced me to people as his brother. "Different fathers, same mother," he'd explain.

I don't think anybody bought it. His skin was dark brown, mine was pink, and we looked nothing alike. Joking aside, we were joined at the hip for several months at the end of our military career.

Both of us grew up in racial melting pots. He had played junior high basketball as the only black kid on an all-white team, and I had been the only white guy on an all-black YMCA team. Coincidence? His parents were faithful to each other, hard workers, good church people, loving and giving to their children, as were mine. They helped him with his homework, went on family camping vacations, modeled their values, and paid only for the essentials. Mine too. Exactly.

Both of our neighborhoods had become less accepting and friendly since we had left home. The civil rights marches of the Fifties and early Sixties had given way to the race riots of the late sixties and early seventies.

"My little cousin has a gun under his bed," Vince explained. "Growing up, we had nothing like this. In Oakland, we weren't raised in fear of each other. Did you have gangs in Sacramento?"

"We had rich on one side of us and poor on the other," I recalled. "I grew up in the middle. I don't remember racial stuff. Of course, being white, I may have been oblivious."

"Wasn't an issue for me, either," Vince agreed. "But, I stayed away from the street. Too much fighting. I guess some of it might have been racial, but I didn't pay attention."

"My folks raised me pretty color-blind," I said. "I remember coming home one day all excited about meeting the parents of one of my buddies. I told my dad that his parents were *Negroes!* At first, he looked shocked at why I would mention their race. Then he hugged me for a long time. It pleased him that I never considered my friend different from me in any way."

"No kidding?" Vince added, "I really get that. When we were kids, we didn't make the distinction."

"His parents were older, so I saw their color."

236

"Very interesting. So, we have to be adults...?"

"Let's agree to never grow *that* old," I suggested.

"Solid, man!"

Walking down a street in Honolulu, we heard the song "He Ain't Heavy, He's My Brother" coming from the external speakers outside a music store. We stood on the sidewalk and sang harmony, belting as loudly as we could. As the song ended, Vince grabbed me in the fireman carry we had learned as medics and lifted me onto his shoulders. For two blocks, as I protested loudly, he continued singing, "He Ain't Heavy, He's My Brother."

When I mentioned we should have a party for my approaching twenty-fourth birthday, Vince said, "My twenty-fourth is next month too." We were stunned to discover that we were both born on April 10, 1946, a mere hundred miles apart, he in Oakland and I in Sacramento.

"I always knew we were twins," I said.

Vince mentioned this coincidence in a letter to his mother, who wrote back that they *lived* in Oakland, but ... "... your father and I had to sneak out of town once in awhile back in the days when we were living with your grandma. Daddy liked to gamble, and your gramma did *not* approve. You weren't due for a few weeks, so I agreed to drive up to Reno with him. I went into labor on the way back. The doctor said it might have been the pressure of the high altitude. We made it as far as Sacramento, and I almost gave birth right there in the car. You were born at Sutter Maternity Hospital about ten minutes after we arrived."

In his next letter, Vince asked his mom why Sutter Maternity had never been mentioned. He said he had been listing Oakland as his "place of birth" as long as he could remember.

She wrote back, "My mother would have had a conniption if she knew we went to Reno. To hide our lie but still visit us in the hospital, your Daddy drove back and forth from Oakland to Sacramento every day for a week."

Vincent's mom continued that she remembered there were only two boy babies in the nursery. "You boys were both so fussy that the nurses had to keep you at opposite ends of the ward so you wouldn't set each other off."

"Well, we finally got together," Vince wrote back.

We threw a two-day birthday bash for forty-eight hours to celebrate our combined forty-eight years. We made copies of our birth certificates and pinned them next to each other on the wall in the kitchen. Several guests asked where we had them made.

"They really look old and authentic."

"These are great! How much did they cost you?"

Most of them refused to believe, no matter what the evidence. Some people simply can't get their mind around synchronicities.

"No, really," I said. "Vince and I were born on the same day in the same hospital. We didn't find out until last month. Sweardagod!"

"Right."

"Sure."

"Of course. Now tell me where you got these printed."

Scatman

Waiting to board the plane, we shook hands, and the actor asked me if my full name was Benjamin.

"Yes, sir."

"Benjamin Sherman?"

"That's what my parents named me," I said.

He smiled. "Pleased to meet you, Benjamin Sherman. You may call me Scat. I don't like sir or mister. Please call me Scat or Scatman."

"Sure, Mr. Scatman," I bowed.

"Hah! I'm going to like you, Benjamin Sherman. You're quick."

In December of 1970, Scatman Crothers joined us on a promotional tour to thirty-two cities in thirty days advertising the premiere of the latest Disney movie. He had dubbed the voice of Scat Cat for *The Aristocats*.

Scatman was my kind of guy – down to earth, humble, gracious, and terminally funny. In a long entertainment career, Scat had worked as a singer and a dancer on stage, a comedian in clubs, and had played supporting roles in many films. Several years later, after I met him on the *Aristocats* promo tour, he starred as Louie the Garbage Man on the TV series *Chico and the Man.*

A promotional tour stood out as a highlight in the life of a Disneyland costumed character. I had toured as Baloo the Bear prior to the premiere of *The Jungle Book*. Now, after my promotion to supervisor, I was asked to direct the *Aristocat* tour. I couldn't say yes fast enough. We traveled in the luxury of the Disney Leer jet, stayed at the best hotels, ate at great restaurants, and were treated like royalty everywhere we went.

Each day in a new city, our schedule was the same. Early in the morning, we appeared on a children's television show, then stayed at the station to appear on a local talk show. After a nice brunch, we did a noon appearance at a shopping mall and spent the afternoon at a children's hospital with photo opportunities for the news media. At each place, Scatman told some family-appropriate jokes, sang his number from the film, and danced with the three costumed cats. In the evening, we appeared in the lobby of a local theater for opening night of the movie. After our brief show, Scat and the cats signed autographs. As soon as the audience had all moved into the auditorium, we hustled the cats into the back of a rental truck where they undressed and packed their costumes while we drove to the airport.

Scat could have been comfortable in the front seat with the driver, but he opted to ride in back with me to help the characters. Not a Hollywood star with the usual ego, Scatman Crothers bonded with all of us right away. We flew to our next city in time for a big meal in a nice restaurant. Usually at about ten o'clock, we went right to bed exhausted. The following day began again at five.

On the plane, Scatman continually entertained us. Having paid his dues on the road, the old hoofer/singer/comic fell into the luxury of our private jet as if a rare privilege had befallen him. He marveled at the amenities and compared them to the cheap motels and highway bistros he had lived in for most of his career.

"Look at this plush upholstery, will ya? I gotta take one of these chairs home with me. I never sat so comfy in my whole life!"

Crothers had an irrepressibly comical mind. He couldn't leave an opening in the air for a second without responding. Being the only person of color on our trip, he used his race as a launching pad for most of his teasing and testing. Race acted as a catalyst, not as a division. We were all who we were, and no one should be the judge. He'd insist that "everybody has a little crazy in them." His humor came from his refusal to take anything or anyone too seriously. He could not give a straight answer, no matter what.

"Scat, if the captain told us that we were going to crash in a minute, you'd find something funny to say," I offered.

"If the captain said we were gonna crash, I'd tell him to get back up there in front where he belongs!" Scat shot back.

"No, I mean …"

"You bet, Benjamin Sherman. But, really, how else would you want to die, if not laughing?"

In route, we played a lot of poker. Scat had all the cards and all the luck. It may have been slight-of-hand cheating, which I wouldn't put past him. He called the games, told jokes, dealt the cards, told more jokes, led the betting, and took our chips, all in one motion. Thirty cities and thirty games later, I had no pocket money. I had learned my lesson to never gamble at cards with a practiced magician.

One night, after his fifth non-stop joke, I grew impatient and wanted him to deal another hand of poker. He held the deck in his fist, waving it around to demonstrate, but none of the cards were hitting the table.

"Come on, Scat," I begged. "Start something."

"Your brother's a moron," he snapped.

"I don't have a brother."

"I say you do. You're a liar and he's a moron."

He tilted his head back and howled. Scat's infectious laugh masked my slow response.

"Oh, I get it," I said sheepishly. "Start something."

Scatman always called me by my full given name, never Ben. He always used the whole thing. I didn't ask him why. A couple of times, when he called me Benjamin

Sherman, I said "OK, Scatman Crothers," but he reacted as if I might be mocking him, so I quit.

"Benjamin Sherman," he'd say. "What shall we have for dinner?"

"The bet is to your two kings, Benjamin Sherman."

"Tell me, Benjamin Sherman, where are you from?"

He even did it when not talking directly to me. I would hear Scat say, "Don't ask me. Better ask Benjamin Sherman."

It had to be some kind of scam, so I ignored it. I got accustomed to my full name, hearing it fifty times a day. Deferring to his stardom, I let it go. I may have even liked it. We had something special between us. He didn't do it with anybody else.

As the trip ended and we landed at the Orange County Airport, I told Scatman how pleased we all were to have him along on the trip.

"I can't imagine that we'd have had this much fun with Ava Gabor or Phil Harris," I assured him.

"Thank you, Benjamin Sherman. Y'all been pleasant company as well. As far as I can tell, nothing of mine has been stolen. Hope we can do this again."

He walked toward his waiting limo. I probably wouldn't see him again.

"OK, I'll bite," I hollered.

He stopped, "Say what?"

"Why always Benjamin Sherman?" I asked.

He walked back to me, smiling broadly. He pulled a wallet out of his breast pocket from which he removed his driver's license. He handed it to me nodding his head.

The name on his license said "Benjamin Sherman Crothers."

Sweardagod.

242

Goofy

In summer of '68, while I played Goofy, a lady stuck a hatpin in the back of my knee. Sweardagod.

Pluto and I were pretending to be statues in the entry of Sleeping Beauty's castle. I guess the old lady wanted to see if I was real. She stuck me pretty hard. As I crumpled to the ground, grabbing at the back of my calf, she realized her foolishness and fled. Pluto saw the whole thing. He ran over to me thinking she had stabbed me with a knife.

A crowd formed. They had no idea what happened, just that Goofy was acting silly as usual. We knew we couldn't take my pants off to investigate in front of all those people, and I couldn't walk or even crawl, so Pluto ran and got security. When they returned, two security officers put me between their shoulders and carried me, legs dragging, to the Fantasyland break area.

There was nothing but a tiny dot visible. No blood. No pin. But, most of the muscles in my leg were now cramping painfully. We waited together for an ambulance. One of the officers brought me a cup of ice, but it was too painful to allow anything to touch the wound.

At the hospital, the X-rays showed that the long pin had lodged in the joint and the head had clipped off. There are a bunch of muscles, tendons, bone and cartilage behind the knee, and they had tightening around the foreign object. It had to be surgically removed.

People look at costumed characters and see oversized toy stuffed animals. Disneyland characters get punched and kicked a lot. As far as we know, however, this was the first time one got stabbed.

It was a mess. Unable to walk at all for a few days, I needed convalescence. My friend Lee and I drove to Las Vegas to try out some new technique he had read about "counting cards." We were pretty lucky and, in two days, we won more than two week's pay.

On the way home, I began talking about life as a professional gambler instead of a pin cushion. Lee and I could skip from casino to casino, from Vegas to Reno to Lake Tahoe, staying one step ahead of anyone from the casinos catching on to our scheme. Facing that Goofy costume again did not sound nearly as romantic as professional gambling.

"My days of Goofy are over," I said.

"You're nuts," Lee responded. "We just got lucky once. You never beat Las Vegas in the long run. And, if they catch us, we'll end up in a dumpster."

As we drove back across the desert, Lee suffered through complaints about my knee, my threats of quitting work first thing in the morning, and fantastic dreams of our new life as gamblers... driving sports cars, smoking long cigars, dating beautiful showgirls...

"I need a break," Lee said.

We stopped at a rest area right before you descend down into the L.A. basin and pulled in next to a guy slowly pouring water over his steaming radiator. The car had Maine plates. His sleeves were rolled to his elbows and sweat stains outlined his armpits and the crease of his back. He looked miserable.

"Long way from home," Lee offered. "Where you headed?"

"Disneyland," he said, more exhausted than enthused. "We've been driving almost nonstop. This is the first trouble I've had with this old heap. The desert heat killed us. Had to keep the windows open and the heater fan going to take heat off the engine. We made it this far and finally lost power. I can't see any leaks. I hope I didn't blow the head gasket."

"Disneyland?" We both asked at once.

"Ah yep. You guys from around there?"

"Sure are."

"We're staying with relatives in Fullerton. Is that anywhere close?"

"Sure," I said. "Right next door. If you're in Fullerton, don't even bother getting back on the freeway. Just take Harbor Boulevard south. Disneyland is on your right after you go over I-5. Six lanes feed the main gate. You can't miss."

"Oh, man, thanks! My directions to my cousin's house take me right down Harbor Boulevard."

"Harbor due south of Fullerton," I repeated.

"I gotta be there first thing in the morning.

"Why the rush?" Lee asked. "You've come this far. Disneyland isn't going anywhere."

"It's my son." He pointed at a boy chasing his sisters. "He's a Goofy fanatic. He's got Goofy dolls, Goofy posters, Goofy T-shirts ... and he's been on my ear all the way across the country. 'When are we going to see Goofy?' every ten minutes. He's making *me* goofy!"

We stood silently. Lee looked at me with a huge smile.

"A friend told me our best chance is very early in the morning, right at the entrance."

"Uh, yeah," I said. "Tomorrow morning at eight o'clock, an hour before they open the Park, they'll let you into Town Square. Goofy hangs out by the Bank of America just through the tunnel on the right side of the big Mickey Mouse planter."

"Wow! Thanks a lot!" he said. "Hey Tommy, you hear that? These guys know where Goofy will be tomorrow!"

His son ran and leaped into his father's arms. "Goofy!" he hollered. "Tomorrow?"

"Tomorrow morning," his dad assured him. He looked at us. "See what I mean?"

"Goofy," Tommy beamed. "I'll never sleep!"

Goofy met his number one fan at a couple of minutes past eight and ducked the whole family under the temporary barrier on Main Street, leaving hundreds of people wondering why these guests were so special. I walked them right down the middle of the street, through the castle, into Fantasyland where I found a few ride operators getting ready to open. We rode alone together on Dumbo, the Tea Cups and the Casey Jr. Train before the Park officially opened. We hit the Matterhorn before the lines started. I took them on Peter Pan, Snow White and Mr. Toad's Wild Ride by walking right to the front and escorting them in as if they were royalty.

We took a dozen pictures and shared many hugs. I walked them over to the launch platform at Small World and waved goodbye until their boat disappeared into the attraction. Tommy blew me a hundred kisses.

It *is* a small world, you know. We're all connected.

Connoisseur

The best way to fall in love is on a long road trip. Of course, I've heard horror stories of good affairs gone wrong because the budding lovers spent too much time in close proximity. It didn't go that way for us. My partnership with my wife started with us driving about three-thousand miles in a small car with a lousy air-conditioner. Sitting side-by-side for countless miles was a prediction for what lay ahead. We have been attached at the hip for twenty-five years through many projects, two children, five mortgages, and several careers.

"I'm going to the west coast for a couple of weeks in June," I said following a nice dinner. "Wanna go?"

"Sure," she said. "I have vacation accumulated."

I really don't know what possessed her to say yes without a thought. It's so unlike her. We had only been dating a little while.

We traveled first to Seattle to visit a friend who took us to the Pike Place Market, up to the top of the Space Needle, to the Ballard Locks, and a dozen other places. The high point of our visit, however, wasn't a usual tourist stop. She took us to a wine-tasting at the obscure Château St. Michelle in a beautiful valley east of Seattle. Our first winery experience left us very impressed. The tour culminated in the tasting room and featured their wine of the day, a '78 Chardonnay.

By this age in my life, I knew wine by twisting a cap, not by removing a cork. My tastes weren't exactly refined. I paid close attention, wanting to appear as sophisticated as I could in the presence of the classy woman at my side. Our host explained that they imported this particular grape from a region of the same name. He pointed to the label on the back of the bottle where the winery had printed side-by-side maps of the State of Washington and the Chardonnay Valley in France, showing that they shared the same latitude.

"The grape vines here enjoy a similar rainfall, sunshine, and year-round barometric pressure as their ancestors in France. It's no wonder that we have such hearty harvests."

He explained that the winter of 1978 had been a bit wetter than most and that spring had come sooner than usual. Those two factors led to a longer season of big juicy Chardonnay grapes. He poured samples, and our tour group agreed that it tasted better than any wine we had experienced. In my case, that was no stretch.

"Chardonnay is the wine of the next generation, the Yuppies," he explained. "Some of you are right in our target age group. You should each buy a whole case of this wonderful wine."

We left with a box of '78 Chardonnay in our trunk. It wasn't cheap, but we were on vacation!

Traveling south to visit my friends and family in California, we stopped in Modesto for dinner with a college chum who worked for Gallo. Now that we were both a little more educated about winemaking, I warned my new girlfriend about my buddy Jim.

"He's a professional wine taster. I bring him wine, and he tells me the variety without looking at the bottle."

"I have to see this," she said.

"We'll take him a bottle of our classy Chardonnay. But, don't say anything about Seattle until after the taste test," I said.

After dinner, Jim swirled the wine in his mouth and pursed his lips, sucking air through his teeth. Not only did he tell us the variety of grape, Chardonnay, but he also knew the winery.

"Were you in Seattle?" he asked.

"Oh my gosh," my companion whispered.

He took another full sip and swallowed appreciatively.

"We can't buy the St. Michelle label down here. They only sell it in Washington. But, I have tasted it several times at competitions. This is truly the best wine you have ever brought me. You see, the Chardonnay Valley in France is the exact same latitude as the vineyards in Woodinville ..."

He went on, repeating almost verbatim the story we had heard two days earlier. I didn't interrupt. I wanted to memorize every word so I could impress my friends. Back in Texas, I recounted my new knowledge every time I opened a bottle of the special wine. As the conversation inevitably moved on to other favorite varietals, I remained quiet. They didn't need to know that my knowledge extended to only one wine from one winery.

Several years later, after we married and had long since finished the case of special Chardonnay, I encountered it again. As the regional director of a professional organization, one of my duties involved finding sites for the regional conferences. Sales and catering managers at nice hotels put me in VIP rooms, and we dined in their best restaurants. This extravagance matched nothing I could afford in my normal life. On a visit to the Fort Worth Hyatt, I noticed Château St. Michelle Chardonnay on the wine list, and I chose it with my dinner.

"You didn't even hesitate," my host observed. "Do you know this wine?"

"Yes. It's my favorite," I said. "Although the '78 is a better year than the '81, as the rainfall came earlier that season in Washington State."

"Oh, my!" she said, smiling at my counterfeit urbane charm.

She invited the wine steward to our table. Fortunately, he didn't ask me to elaborate on my knowledge of other wines. I did tell him all I knew about the Chardonnay grape and the location of its birth, the care by which it was brought to America, the vineyards, the rainfall, and all the information I had gleaned several years earlier at the winery and from Jim. I described the beautiful Woodinville Valley. I waxed eloquently while we each sipped and they warmed themselves by my false fire of intellect.

I took home from Ft. Worth a bottle of my only favorite wine and poured glasses for my wife and some close friends. We all had quite a laugh as I told them about how I had impressed my hosts at the five-star Hyatt with my singular wine story, the one they had heard several times as well.

"Sorry it's an '81," I said.

"Well, drinking by the year is certainly a step up from by the month," my wife observed.

We were mostly beer and margarita people, but we all agreed that we could get accustomed to living in the presidential suites of great hotels. We could learn to eat gourmet food and drink only the finest wines.

Two years later, our regional conference met at the Hyatt in Ft. Worth where I had inked a generous deal by signing an early contract. The hotel again gave me their finest room. When I moved in, I spotted a VIP fruit basket on the table in the suite. To my amazement, the hotel had included a bottle of '78 Château St. Michelle Chardonnay. Yes, 1978. Their best year.

The salesperson with whom I had signed the original contract no longer worked for the hotel. I stood there holding the bottle, dumbfounded.

"They must have one incredible client tracking system," I thought to myself.

The next morning at a breakfast meeting with the new sales manager, I thanked her for her sensitivity in finding my very favorite wine to include with the welcome basket of goodies.

"You must have pretty good notes," I suggested. "It's even a '78."

"Thank you," she responded somewhat perplexed. "But, I have to be honest and say that I had nothing to do with selecting the wine in your basket. That's something the hotel does."

"Interesting," I replied. "Would your wine steward know about my being here?"

"I don't really think so. I haven't met her yet. I can ask."

"Her? The wine steward I met was a man."

"Oh, they change all the time. When were you here?"

The mystery bothered me all day. That evening at dinner in the hotel restaurant, I noticed that Chateau St. Michelle didn't appear on their wine list. The waiter had never heard of that particular brand. When I asked for the wine steward, he said she didn't work that night, but he would talk to the wine buyer.

"The wine buyer?"

"Yes. He lives here in Ft. Worth and eats here at least once a week. I'll find out about the Chardonnay next time he's in. Your conference is here for the next four days. I'll be sure to get back to you."

The following morning, I asked my sales contact if she knew the Hyatt wine buyer.

"Yes. He works in our corporate office upstairs. When he's in town, I see him often."

"Is he here this week?"

"I'll check. Just a moment."

She called a number, and I could hear a man's voice coming from her earpiece. She smiled and nodded at me as she arranged a short visit. The man who stood up to greet me in his office said with a smile, "Of course, I know Mr. Sherman. We met several years ago in the dining room."

I recognized him as the wine steward to whom I had told my Chardonnay story.

"You were the wine steward then," I said. "Were you promoted?"

"Ah, yes. A bit embarrassing. We were between wine stewards at that moment, and your knowledge of wines left our sales director a bit nervous. She saw me eating with my wife and asked me to fill in. I have always been the wine buyer, never a wine steward."

"I received a bottle of '78 Château St. Michelle in my room. Did that come from you?"

"Oh. No. Not from me, so to speak. That goes in every VIP room, in every Hyatt, worldwide."

"The 1978?"

"Yes, the '78.

"I noticed no Château St. Michelle on your wine list."

"We ran out years ago. I really should buy some more. I guess I'm just waiting for another year like the '78. The others weren't quite as good, as you said. Once you get spoiled on a particular taste, you know …"

"You say you have the '78 for VIP rooms only?

"Yes. After talking with you and hearing your intriguing story of the matching latitudes, I flew directly to Seattle."

"Woodinville?"

"Exactly! Woodinville. Lovely winery. That whole area. Lush green. I drove out and met with their entire staff. They were very hospitable. We toured the vineyards. I saw the little print shop where they make the labels. I had a memorable visit. You know, they are right about that valley looking and feeling much like the Chardonnay Valley in France."

"And you bought…?"

"Every single case. I could not have been more impressed. Chardonnay soon became popular all over the world, and I felt like I had the jump on one of the best. Great bragging rights in my circle, to be sure."

"Every case?"

"I bought the whole production."

"On my say?"

"You were right, Mr. Sherman. You definitely know your wines. What are your thoughts today? Have you come to give me another great lead?"

I backed out, bowing, making excuses about being late for a meeting, begging his pardon. I sat in my room for a long time just taking deep breaths before I could call my wife to share the story and a long laugh.

A dozen years later, I lived near Seattle and ran a consulting business. Subsequently, I found myself in the boardroom of Château St. Michelle in Woodinville, Washington. They hired me to facilitate an annual strategic planning session for their directors. We completed our work a bit early, and I asked permission to tell them a personal story about my connection with their winery.

I told a rapt audience about my first visit, the wine tasting, about my friend Jim in Modesto who worked for Gallo, and about the whole sequence of events that led to my final meeting with the Hyatt's wine buyer.

"That is an interesting story," an old man in the back said. "What year again?"

"We were here in summer of '81 and that would have been the next spring. So, about March or April of 1982."

"Most of you weren't here then. We were facing tough times."

I realized the man speaking must be the owner or president.

"We had over-extended ourselves in '78 because of the lushness of those grapes. We knew we had an exquisite once-in-a-lifetime wine, but we had no capacity to sell everything we made. We were paying to warehouse it while borrowing heavily to defray the tremendous production costs. Sadly, we weren't as good at marketing as we were at making wine. That wonderful wine just sat there collecting dust. Then, that sale to the Hyatt happened and doubled our profits in 1982."

The president took a breath and let out a long sigh. He looked back at me. "So, you're the guy who saved our little winery."

"God sells in mysterious ways," I said.

Postscript

My mom taught me to dance.
"Don't look at your feet!" she'd say, gently tapping
under my chin. "Look where we're going instead of down."
I'd miss a step and look down again. She'd patiently
explain to me, "I'm backing up most of the time. I need you
to watch for traffic. Our feet will follow along under us
without you watching them."
What a wonderful metaphor for life. It's amazing what
you might miss if you stop looking ahead.
"Are all these stories really true?" people ask me.
"Yes."
"Why do you think so many crazy things happen to
you?"
"They happen to everyone. I just don't watch my feet."
Keep your chin up and keep watching. Something
wonderful is bound to happen. Sweardagod.